HOLLYWOOD

Land and Legend

By

ZELDA CINI AND BOB CRANE
WITH PETER H. BROWN

ARLINGTON HOUSE
WESTPORT, CONNECTICUT

This book was produced for Arlington House/Publishers by

 Rosebud Books Inc.
8777 Lookout Mountain Avenue
Los Angeles, California 90046

Jacket and book design by Michael Burke

Library of Congress Cataloging in Publication Data

Cini, Zelda.
  Hollywood, land & legend.

  1. Hollywood, Calif.—History. 2. Moving-pictures—United States—History. 3. Moving-picture actors and actresses—United States—Biography. I. Crane, Bob., 1927-   joint author. II. Brown, Peter, 1939-   joint author. III. Title.
F869.H74C56   979.4′94   80-23933
ISBN: 0-87000-486-7

DEDICATION

To Zelda, who, better than any
of us, loved and understood Hollywood
for what it was, and, even more,
for what it wasn't.
We and Hollywood will miss her.

ACKNOWLEDGEMENTS
Many people have contributed to the making of this book.
The authors would like to thank the Academy of Motion
Picture Arts and Sciences, Don Ackland, Sue Atkinson,
Bunny Berkley, Alan Berliner, Larry Brooks, Pamela Brown,
Michael Burke, California Historical Society, Elissa Collins,
Carole Epstein, Douglas Fairbanks, Jr., Rick Frey, Bo
Hathaway, Terry Helgesen, Bruce Henstell, Ruth Murray
Reid, William Wallace Reid, Bernard Schleifer, Anthony
Slide, Bruce Torrance, Rudy Vallee, Marc Wanamaker of
Bison Archives and Dick Whittington.

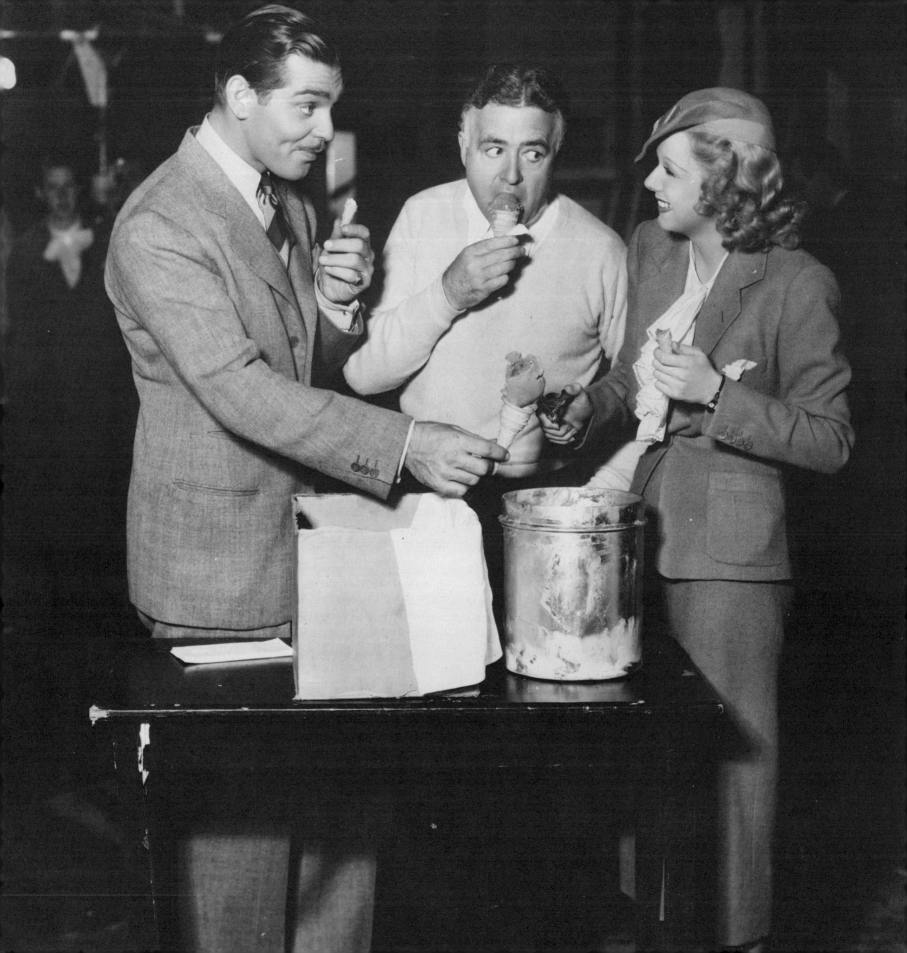

Contents

She called him "King" and he called her "baby," and the relationship between Clark Gable and Jean Harlow (here with ice cream on the set of Saratoga, 1937) was one of rare warmth in Hollywood's rat warren of envy and ambition. A month after this photo was taken, Harlow died a mysterious death. "The best pal I had in this town was a dame," said Gable . . . "Too fragile for us."

List of Illustrations

Photo Credits

An over-idealistic H.H. Wilcox ordered this map made as the blueprint for the Hollywood he saw in his mind—an orderly, sedate, country club community of "the best people." "And then we came," said Cecil B. De Mille. "And Wilcox saw his dream disappear the minute the first camera crews came in. Show People! What a disaster."

Three early tourists from the East pick their fill of casaba melons from an isolated field that is now the Eastern edge of the Sunset Strip. (Harper Avenue and Sunset Boulevard.) The year was 1918 and you still had to take a rutted road two miles from the pavement. Within five years the Gothic palaces of the Hollywood hills appeared on the knolls and melons had to be trucked in from distant El Centro.

I WHAT'S HOLLYWOOD?
From Figwood to Film Capital

For people who have never been to Hollywood, the name itself is something to conjure with. Actually, "conjure" is the perfect way to deal with Hollywood, for it was born in fantasy and nourished on the magic of the silver screen.

Everything about the place defies logic, even its name. Holly doesn't grow in Hollywood. Never did. Figs grow in Hollywood. So do citrus fruits. And apricots, loquats, guavas, grapes, melons, and avocados. Even banana palms grow in Hollywood, although the fruit is really not edible. But holly simply doesn't take root.

Still, when the husband of Daeida Hartell Wilcox built a country house in the middle of a fig orchard, she christened it Hollywood because she liked the name of an Illinois estate rimmed by holly trees. And that's the truth.

Eventually, of course, the fig orchard became a subdivision which in turn became a city in 1903. At that, it was only Sixth Class and didn't last. In 1910 the people of Hollywood changed their minds and voted to become a part of Los Angeles. And that's all it is today—"a northwest sector of the city of Los Angeles."

11

That's the truth, too.

So, it isn't a city. It doesn't grow holly. And it isn't even a fig orchard anymore.

Then what is Hollywood?

Hollywood is a place. It's Camelot and the Blarney Stone. It attracts equal numbers of knights in shining armor, beauteous ladies, rapacious villains, artists, leprechauns, and beggars.

Hollywood is a place which has always had more than its share of dope pushers, pimps, and prostitutes, but it has also been a place canopied by a semicircular black sky pierced by fingers of light from Otto K. Oleson's "arc lights."

In the days of elaborate premières, from the beach cities ten miles away on the west to conservative Pasadena on the east, those moving arrows of light were provocative reminders of the glamour so nearby—and so untouchably far away.

On Hollywood Boulevard, even before the sun had set, the royal red carpet had been rolled out from the shadowy entrance to the Chinese Theatre all the way to the curb, where limousines would roll up, discharge their elegantly-clad passengers and be waved away to accommodate the flow of mirror-image duplicates.

On both sides of the rich velvet carpet, tiers of hastily-erected bleachers were crowded to the point of collapse by eager movie fans willing to endure even bad weather for a quick glimpse of the stars from that other world, the distant realm of fantasy.

(Above)
Transportation made the difference between an isolated village and the city it was to become. By 1887, the L.A. County Railroad traveled west from downtown Los Angeles along Sunset Avenue (now Boulevard), disgorging passengers at Sisters' Hospital near Vermont Avenue. The Southern Pacific Railroad was also huffing and puffing eastward and west again, contributing weekly to the continuing influx of migrants who finally settled in Hollywood.

(Right)
Like an eye in the middle of the hurricane, a few rural oases—such as this one—were still untouched in the Hollywood of 1926, a Hollywood that was already being called the modern "Sodom" or "Gomorrah" (depending on the author). These two horses are clearing a hillock for a Lloyd Wright house at 5121 Franklin Avenue.

(Opposite, top)
Sunset Boulevard in 1900 was only a tree-shaded country road, inches thick in dust in the summer, floating in mud during the rainy season. This photo, taking a westerly view from the Normandie Avenue intersection (marker post at left) shows the easternmost boundary of the city to come.

(Opposite, left)
In 1896, Sunset Boulevard meandered northward towards Western Avenue, edged by young trees ingeniously kept alive during months of drought by the moisture from broken melons packed down at the roots.

Jacob Miller, whose interest in farming extended to the importation of avocado trees from Guatemala and coffee trees from South America, wasted no time in building a comfortable home and barn at Hollywood Boulevard and Nichols Canyon Road about 1884. Bordering on Hancock's share of Rancho La Brea, up to and including the central section of the Plummer ranch, the whole area west of Wilcox's Hollywood project to where Doheny Avenue is today is now most logically called West Hollywood.

Especially during the Great Depression of the thirties, when even food for ordinary people was hard to come by, the flaunted affluence of the movie star somehow restored one's faith in the potentials of "free enterprise."

In the dark and fragrant confines of Grauman's Chinese Theatre on Hollywood Boulevard, patrons were directed to their seats by lavishly-costumed ushers in Oriental brocades. When a hush finally settled over this privileged audience, the screen came alive with larger-than-life dramas of soul-wrenching conflict. But the villain was always punished, the hero won his lady and together they sailed off into the sunset, or set the sky aflame with fireworks as they kissed, or simply got married and lived happily ever after.

Outside, the fans in the bleachers waited for the film to end. Flash bulbs popped, momentarily blinding their victims. Local and network radio announcers described the scene in vivid detail, catching stars on the wing for ad lib interviews. Newspaper and magazine reporters rushed madly to their own cars, parked blocks away, and raced away to meet deadlines for their various editions, filing mostly prewritten press agent handouts freely provided by the studios. Production stills, posed and shot in studio photo galleries, had long ago met fan magazine deadlines. Movie columnists, like Hedda Hopper, Louella Parsons, and Walter Winchell, drifted toward their own limousines amid the crush of press agents hoping to plant still another item to build another movie name through the syndicated gossip pieces which had

Major H. M. Mitchell, attorney and Nichols Canyon bee rancher who fired the shot that felled the bandit Tiburcio Vasquez, had every reason to believe he would live a long and prosperous life. He served as Los Angeles County Sheriff from 1878–79, when he was admitted to practice before the Supreme Court of California. A few years later, however, by an ironic twist of fate, while hunting near the scene of the Vasquez capture he was mistaken for a deer and fatally shot—by a friend.

Cecil's Indians they were called—a rag-tag pot-luck gaggle of refugees from a dozen wild-west shows. Cecil B. De Mille trucked them out for 1913's The Squaw Man, the first feature filmed entirely in Hollywood. De Mille hadn't meant to make the film out West. It's just that he spent all the location money on a sultan's trip across America. So with what was left he settled down in the California sun.

This Victorian masterpiece at Laurel Canyon and Sunset boulevards in 1905 was at the very height of Cape Cod fashion—with a sleeping porch, cellar, cold room for meats, orange groves, raspberry hedges, and bee hives. Furthermore, the quiet, sane atmosphere so prized by Victorians was de rigueur here. Not for long, though; by 1925 a speakeasy with Chinese lanterns swinging from the porch would flourish a scant block away. And Hollywood's earliest settlers—prohibitionists all, would be driven to Northern California. "The movies," lamented pioneer Eleanor Cole. "The riff raff engulfed us." And, ironically, that line formed the plot for an early silent—Riff-Raff.

probably gone to press hours, even days, before, depending upon editorial whim or political pressure.

After the première, the shiny chauffeur-driven limousines paraded westward and slightly south to Sunset Boulevard, where Ciro's, the Troc, and Mocambo awaited the usual influx.

Again, in relatively orderly lines on both sides of the entrance doors, eager fans awaited—to look. Not touch. Not grab at the clothes, as they were likely to do years later. Just to stand back and gape at the furs, the jewels, the elegance, the attentiveness of the handsome males, many of whom were also stars.

Never did it occur to an ardent fan that tomorrow's shooting was scheduled. That the stars were expected to report to makeup at 5 a.m., fresh and line-ready. That their shoes, borrowed from studio wardrobe, were too tight, or that they hated the beautiful lady they were obliged to escort and that she returned the emotion—in spades.

"My God, almost anything we do here will be an improvement," said John Barrymore who was scouting for a hilltop home in 1915. And this view of Hollywood from Lookout Mountain shows what the thespian meant. Scruffy eucalyptus, unedible cactus and sticker weeds decorated the early landscape. But in 1930 after the movies put the city on the map, pioneers would bemoan this Paradise Lost.

They were all victims of the "star system," that quiet substratum which allowed these "animals," these "properties," less freedom than that accorded the studio watchdog, that snarling protective companion of the night guard at the locked gates of the darkened studio itself.

The stars? Creations all, contrived for perfection, mouthing dialogue beautifully, under proper direction. Standing or sitting interminably for stills, fan photos, and the right key-lights on the set. Watching their weight. Taking pills (on studio doctors' prescriptions) to sleep by, and pills for waking up. Living out their limited little lives as movie stars in protective custody, doing what they were told to do, so long as they and their contracts both should live.

Outside the studio gates, there was Hollywood. Most of the studios weren't in Hollywood. They were in the San Fernando Valley—in North Hollywood, Studio City, Burbank. They still are. They were in Culver City, southwest of Hollywood, in a shabby middle-class com-

Hollywood in 1910 with the famous fruit-growing belts—the Cahuenga, Laurel, and Hollywood valleys stretching up into the still-nude hills. The houses are Victorian clapboard; the gardens are late London townhouse. But this staid English look was carefully planned; in the gorges where Spanish land-grant caballeros had chased bandits, the new developers of Hollywood were determined to erect a city built on Christian ethics; a city with no red-light district and, my lands, no theater people. "The approach to Los Angeles was impressive," said MGM writer Frances Marion, one of the first true scriptwriters of the silents. "Hundreds of acres abounded with orange and lemon groves—a heaven on earth." After Miss Marion got off the train, she noticed both the heat of the city and the coolness of its residents to "stage folks." "I decided to find an apartment that I could convert into a studio of sorts," she said. "And there were plenty of vacancies. But over each rental sign was the wording 'No Jews, actors or dogs allowed.' What an insult this was—after coming from New York where Jews are revered for their contributions and actors are as welcome as the holidays." Marion walked through the streets of the town—in the exact year of this panorama—and cased the prospects. Then she pulled out her diary and scrawled: "What a provincial town this is. I'll finish my job in a hurry; clear out of here; and never come back!"

munity which made no claims to glamour. They're still there, too.

In Hollywood itself, there was Gower Gulch—the corner of Sunset Boulevard and Gower Street where Hollywood's first films were made in 1911. Here was an area which, by the forties, had progressed all the way downward to where it had begun—to "quickie" westerns—and whatever elaborate musicals Columbia Pictures decided to make. Nearby, on Santa Monica Boulevard, Goldwyn Studios were also in full operation, partly on a rent-out basis for independent productions. Near Goldwyn, as if for protection, there was General Service Studios, available to any producer with the financing and the will to make an independent film. Eastward, on Melrose Avenue, there was Paramount, DeMille Productions, and RKO, which Howard Hughes owned and sometimes used for moviemaking.

Chaplin Studios, never overly active, still occupied its original acreage at the corner of La Brea Avenue and Sunset Boulevard, not far from where Greek George the Camel Herder had grazed his strange beasts a few decades before.

Sunset Boulevard, an anomaly from start to finish, was a four-lane highway which absorbed Hollywood Boulevard on the east at New Hampshire Avenue in Los Angeles for starters. On the west, it became an erratically winding route all the way to the Pacific Coast Highway and the sea. Nothing wrong with that.

Except, maybe, that on its way through Hollywood it slid past

luxurious restaurants and night clubs, coffee shops and all-night sand-wich joints. It wound through West Hollywood's false-fronted gambling spots, steam baths, massage parlors, and burlesque houses. Every bar had its friendly bartenders who knew everybody and, for a price, readily arranged for lonely men to meet pretty girls, and pretty girls to meet rich and handsome producers who could cut through the hardships and set them into starring roles in movies which were, unfortunately, not quite ready to go into production, for one reason or another.

On any sunny weekend afternoon, the winding boulevard was spotted at strategic intersections with hawkers, a strange breed indig-enous to Hollywood, devoted to selling maps of movie-stars' homes to gullible tourists. At best, the maps were inaccurate. At worst, they were total fabrications. But tour buses did travel past the mansions in the Hollywood and Bel-Air hills, eastward to Chateau Marmont just north of Sunset Boulevard, where almost every movie star, writer, director, and producer in the film industry since the twenties lived at some time, and still does, however briefly. The nearby Garden of Allah across the street was similarly blessed with famous names. So was Sunset Towers, one of Hollywood's earliest highrise apartments with a rooftop swim-ming pool and a breathtaking view of the south valley below.

Hollywood Boulevard, on the other hand, only a couple of blocks north of Sunset and parallel to it, starts suddenly at Laurel Canyon Boulevard as a wide residential street, narrows slightly at La Brea Ave-

This panoramic photograph of the Hollywood hills is continued on page 20 and 21. Taken thirteen years before the Hollywoodland sign was erected on Mount Lee (center above), this photograph traverses from left to right: The Cahuenga Pass, Mount Lee, Mount Hollywood, Griffith Park, Los Feliz, Chavez Ravine and Glendale.

The homes shown in this panorama were occupied by quiet couples from the East who had come to retire in this sleepy town with its wisteria- and lemon-scented nights. By 1911 the city fathers had banned everything they could think of that would lower the tone: slaughterhouses, gasworks, textile mills, even the cultivation of cotton with its hordes of laborers. But they overlooked the movie people—preferring instead to ban alcohol in any form. "Franklin Avenue in those days was arched with pepper branches and Vine Street was covered over with both peppers and palms," said Agnes De Mille, whose father William was Cecil B. De Mille's brother and one of the first of the movie executives to move out to Hollywood. "Sunset Boulevard snaked through the hills, following an old cattle trail, and petered out long before the coast. For some of its length, a bridle path ran down the center—with horses being the most sensible method of transportation in Hollywood." It's safe to assume that the neighborhoods in this tranquil photo were literally "closed" to the "movies" as film people were called then. Even Lillian Gish, a blue blood from the East along with her sister Dorothy and her mother, found it almost impossible to get lodgings. Finally they settled for a boarding house in old Los Angeles—far from the more exclusive Hollywood. The studios were only ramshackle buildings and the stages were little more than platforms. There were no movie offices because all the money men and the salesmen had stayed in New York. "I really didn't expect the movies to stay out here," said Frances Marion. "Nobody wanted us, and the city was so incredibly stuffy."

nue and proceeds sedately northward as a business boulevard lined with shops, more movie houses, etc. Even the casual observer could recognize the Chinese, Egyptian, Paramount, Warner's Fox, Pantages, Academy, and other movie houses, and suddenly, Hollywood Wax Museum, where stars are frozen, fully-costumed and lifelike, in flesh-colored wax.

Traffic is heavy in Hollywood, on every street and boulevard. It has to be heavy. Not only hasn't there been any adequate public transportation since the trolley tracks were ripped out in the late forties and early fifties (when they were most needed) to make way for freeways, but the two million tourists that Hollywood attracts each year further compound the clutter.

In the late twenties, Frank Lloyd Wright, the revolutionary designer-architect, told a group of people that in his view the "Continental Tilt" was a phenomenon which made it possible for all loose nuts in the United States to slide into Hollywood.

Why Hollywood? What is there about this northwest sector of the city of Los Angeles that exerts such a magnetic attraction on so many people who seem to have absolutely nothing else in common?

Maybe it's the weather—mild, warm, dry. But there are also periods of torrential rain, excessive desert heat, occasional drought, Santa Ana winds, "unusual" frost, and earthquakes.

The hills? They're pretty. The people who live there are known

as a snobbish fraternity of "hill people." To them, everybody else is a "flatlander."

Hollywood is, of course, partially framed by hills on the north and north-east. On the south, and toward the west, the terrain tends to flatten out, which is scarcely enough to justify the survival of Hollywood and the total demise of the adjacent community of Colegrove.

In the earliest days of landgrabs and subdivisions, a U.S. senator named Cornelius Cole tried valiantly to make a durable community out of Colegrove, a subdivision he had created from his own acreage adjoining Hollywood on the south.

He had contributed generously to the development of a local railway system near his property; built a nine-hole golf course, the first in the area; and even established an exclusive tennis club for added social status.

Nonetheless, in the countywide hassle over water, Colegrove, like Hollywood, was absorbed into the city of Los Angeles. Unlike Hollywood, however, it disappeared without a trace. The people of Colegrove, devastated by its demise, made a mighty effort to retain some form of identity by suggesting that, as a concomitant of annexation, the area should hereinafter be known as South Hollywood. It was so ordered—but the name died aborning. Nobody paid attention.

On the other hand, Hollywood, in defiance of any logical explanation, continued to grow, the name gaining momentum as North

Five hundred rose bushes, a thousand tulip bulbs, armloads of jonquils, and fifty bloom-bearing trees created a Hollywood Eden for impressionistic artist Paul De Longpré—here with his daughter on a Sunday morning. But Hollywood producers took no lesson from this artificial paradise. When the movie men built their studios and office buildings they routinely chopped down the eucalyptus, hibiscus, and myrtle trees, creating a land of concrete—the first suburbia.

De Longpré's Mansion, architecturally compatible with his nearby Moorish studio, was built in 1902 on the corner of Hollywood and Cahuenga boulevards after Mrs. Beveridge had deeded the property to him, in exchange for three original De Longpré paintings in lieu of the $3,000 asking price. In addition, the Beveridges had obligingly moved their own home off the property and relocated it a block away—on the corner of Cahuenga and Yucca avenues. By the end of the following year the press had made the artist, his palatial 3½-acre estate, his lavish parties, and Hollywood, where all this action was, glamorously world famous.

Hollywood, miles away on the San Fernando Valley side of the old Cahuenga Pass, emerged and flourished. So did that meandering slice of Los Angeles County now known as West Hollywood, which was originally named Sherman in honor of the General who first built the railway and the essential housing for his laborers.

Each "Hollywood" has a quality of its own, and did from the beginning. North Hollywood, which had acquired a toehold on the moviemaking business in the first decade of the twentieth century with the establishment of Universal City, seemed predestined to become a provincial, almost rural, community surrounding a spate of movie studios.

West Hollywood, with no city ordinances to deal with and geographically isolated from city and county law-enforcement agencies, by whatever name, had held its beginnings as the outer edge of Rancho La Brea. It was in the relative security of this area that Hollywood's most romantic bandit, Tiburcio Vasquez, hid out; and fifty years later, Mobster Mickey Cohen conducted his thriving gambling and prostitution business from the back room of an otherwise innocent-appearing haberdashery store.

As for Hollywood itself, except for the fact that it had been widely touted in national land sales and railroad train promotions as

In West Hollywood in 1889, typical of the agricultural output in what was then known as "the north valley," which included all of Hollywood and Colegrove, as well, was this portion of the Hammel and Denker farm planted in peas. In September 1889 a serious group of dirt-farmers met to form "The Farmers' League of Cahuenga Township," a cooperative association for the marketing of vegetables and semitropical fruits in Los Angeles and San Francisco. A survey of the period showed that in this area alone there were 291 acres of tomatoes, 102 acres of peas, 82 acres of beans, and 20 acres of chilis, exclusive of the fruit orchards which dominated the landscape.

The Hollywood Hotel at the corner of Hollywood Boulevard and Highland Avenue was the setting for a continuing round of meetings and celebrations following the formation of the city of Hollywood in 1903.

Hollywood's first general store was the property of John Watts, an English dry-goods clerk who landed in Los Angeles in 1886 and promptly bought a general merchandising store at the corner of Vine Street and Santa Monica Avenue (now Boulevard). In 1895 he returned to England, possibly because he had tired of the tradition which permitted regular customers to dip into a village merchant's cashbox for emergency loans, leaving IOUs for the record.

"the frostless belt" enjoying "sunshine 350 days per year," only coincidence could have made it what it is. Only the wishful thinking of a world of innocents and the creative talents of well-paid press agents could have transformed a subdivided fig ranch into a Sixth Class City compacted into twenty-four square miles, and then produced from it "the motion picture capital of the world."

Truth of the matter is, movies were being made in Palo Alto, California, before 1880, very, very, experimentally. They were also being made in Los Angeles, Chatsworth, and Santa Barbara, before any of the early filmmakers were aware of the existence of a place called Hollywood.

The earliest moviemakers, in flight from New Jersey where their infringements on the patents of Thomas Edison were putting them all in imminent danger of free room and board in the pokey, perhaps unwittingly set the moral tone of this extraordinary industry for generations to come.

Like the name itself, which never had validity, Hollywood has become the generic term for wherever movies are made. It is rarely used without an essential modifier, "glamorous."

Hollywood's first hotel, a three-story wood structure with eighteen bedrooms and one bath, was built about 1888 by Horace D. Sackett on three sixty-five-foot lots facing Cahuenga Boulevard at the southwest corner of Hollywood Boulevard. Sackett himself, whose forebearers had arrived in America from England in 1631 and who was a descendant of one of the eight founding families of Cambridge, Massachusetts, had disposed of a general store in Suffield, Connecticut, and arrived in Hollywood in 1887 with his wife, five children, and $10,000. By 1897 his hotel, with its "culinary department," general store (Hollywood's second) and upstairs offices, had also become the local post office. Not until 1905, after Philo J. Beveridge had become postmaster, with Sackett's daughter Mary as his assistant, did this mail service relocate into its own building. Meanwhile, however, it did lend official credibility to the place called Hollywood. Until then, mail delivery at best was erratic. Common practice provided that mail be dropped into fruit crates near the door, where it was assumed the addressee collected only that correspondence which was rightfully his.

Spring storm clouds off the Pacific drift dramatically behind the Arthur Letts' mansion on Franklin Avenue at Western, where Letts fashioned his own empire—free, he thought, from the materialism and progress of the East. Letts could hardly have known that a struggling actor-director named Cecil B. De Mille was already at work only half a mile away on Hollywood's first really big film, The Squaw Man. *The year was 1913.*

Early undated photo of Curzon Terrace, probably very early 1900s. From the width of this road, it is only logical to assume that any vehicle, having made it to the top, either never came down again or knew how to handle the inevitability of stalemate!

A stagecoach road left over from the Spanish Trail was the only route between Hollywood and the San Fernando Valley. But it didn't really matter because there was nothing in the valley anyway—not even water. These bikers of summer 1897 must have been out for the exercise across the Cahuenga Pass, which is now sealed beneath a thousand tons of concrete.

In California, on a clear night or day, its only identifying sign may be seen high in the hills from miles away—and even that has no validity. It is now a steel replacement for a rotted wooden advertising sign locating a 1926 canyon subdivision called Hollywoodland. Ironically, the "land" part of the sign was the first to tear loose from its moorings and slide downhill, leaving only "Hollywood."

Ironically, too, behind that Hollywoodland development was a man, publisher of the Los Angeles *Times,* whose efforts on behalf of a poorly-qualified dam builder named William Mulholland, stripped Hollywood of its identity as a city and forced its annexation to the city of Los Angeles. Even then, although Hollywood didn't exist, it didn't disappear either.

Maybe it isn't a place after all. Maybe it never was.

Maybe Hollywood itself is a fantasy and only the people who created it have substance. In any event, that's what this book is about— the people of Hollywood and how they left their marks on the space they occupied.

POLICE STATION.

131

II THE PASSING FRONTIER: 1875 to 1910
The First Studio

It took most of a leisurely afternoon in 1908 to travel on this Pacific Electric trolley car from downtown Los Angeles to the intersection of Sunset and Laurel Canyon boulevards (shown here). But a year later, September 23, 1909, the construction of the Hill Street tunnel cut a precious twelve minutes off the traveling time and, thus, created Hollywood's first building boom. The mansions in the background were hung with bunting and even General Otis opened his house to nosy tourists. Of course nobody then, not even Paul De Longpré, imagined that tourism would be the only grace left to a less charming, urbanized Hollywood in 1980.

Flower-framed slammer (ca. 1910) sat prettily on Cahuenga Boulvard, between Hollywood Boulevard and Selma Avenue, conveniently central as the temporary residence of anybody who got caught with alcoholic beverages, in him or on him. One of the city's very first ordinances absolutely forbade "intoxicating beverages."

Everybody knows the name, but very few people know precisely what Hollywood is, or even where it is. . . .

"Hollywood," according to the Random House Unabridged Dictionary, is "the NW part of Los Angeles, CA., center of the motion picture industry," and "a city in SE Florida, near Miami." End of item.

For purposes of this book, forget Florida, but not before you notice that at least Florida's Hollywood is a city. California's Hollywood is not.

California's Hollywood has no city limits, no courthouse, no city hall, although it does have a Chamber of Commerce. On the other hand, so does West Hollywood, which isn't a city either, nor does it belong to one. It belongs solely to Los Angeles County, of which Hollywood is also a part. Unlike Los Angeles (El Pueblo Grande) which was founded quite traditionally on September 4, 1781, by forty-four settlers (two Spaniards, twenty-six blacks, sixteen assorted Indians and *mestizos*), Hollywood owes its beginnings, a full century later, to two settlers, a Mr. and Mrs. Harvey Henderson Wilcox of Topeka, Kansas.

Harvey Wilcox was fifty-one when he arrived in Los Angeles

Vasquez and his Captors.

It took a posse of seven to capture the elusive outlaw, Tiburcio Vasquez, who was quietly enjoying breakfast unarmed and alone, with only the slim form of a native girl between him and the heavily-armed men who stopped his attempt to escape by shooting him in the shoulder and peppering the rest of his body with buckshot. Hauled off to jail in the back of a wagon on May 15, 1874, he was subsequently tried, convicted and hanged in Monterrey County on March 19, 1875.

Greek George the camel herder first befriended and then betrayed the bandit Tiburcio Vasquez when the $15,000 reward for his capture became irresistible. But even without Vasquez, Greek George would have carved a niche for himself in the annals of early Hollywood, for it was he who led the camels which hauled supplies to build the Butterfield Route for the Overland Mail Company. The longest continuous stage-line ever established, it stretched from St. Louis to Los Angeles, covered 2,880 miles and was completed in September 1858. Twenty days later the first mail coach arrived, carrying one passenger: W. L. Ormsby, a reporter for the New York Herald.

with two pinto horses, a black coachman, and a bride, twenty-one-year-old Daeida, his second wife.

Daeida Hartell had married Harvey Wilcox three years after his first wife had died, despite the disparity in their ages and a few other minor drawbacks.

He was also a paraplegic, paralyzed in both legs by polio at sixteen. Nonetheless, he had determinedly developed partial use of the upper part of one leg, enough at least to enable him to get around on crutches.

After graduation from Michigan's Adrian College with honors, Wilcox migrated to Bryan, Ohio, where he became county recorder, an elected office, and where he met and married his first wife. Together they moved on to Topeka, Kansas, where he plunged headlong into the real estate business and supported the enactment of a Kansas law which forbade the sale of intoxicating beverages in that state thirty years before the rest of the U.S. had even thought of prohibition.

He also became extremely wealthy, permitting himself the purchase of a fine pair of pinto horses which he named "Duke" and "Royal." Then at the peak of his success, he was widowed . . . until Daeida came along.

The newlyweds jumped a train to Los Angeles, and Wilcox quickly put his idle money to work. He opened an office at 134 South Spring Street (now the Los Angeles *Times* building), ensconced his bride in a spacious town house nearby, and proceeded to buy, subdivide, and sell the most attractive acreage on the borders of the city. Then, on Sundays, with Duke and Royal hitched to the carriage, the Wilcoxes drove farther and farther afield exploring wide stretches of land for possible investment.

On just such an afternoon, early in 1886, Daeida spotted a fruit ranch framed on one side by the gentle slopes of the Cahuenga Mountains. A half-day's drive northwest of Los Angeles, row upon row of fig trees covered most of this 120-acre plot of flatland—and Daeida wanted it for her very own. So, Harvey bought it—for an estimated $300 cash.

Even before Harvey had grown accustomed to this investment, Daeida had convinced him that a lovely country home was absolutely essential to her happiness. Once more he indulged her, beginning construction almost immediately. Why not? He was reaping the rewards of one of the biggest land booms in southern California history.

For whatever reasons, in the midst of construction on her new home, Daeida decided to go back to Topeka for a visit.

That visit may have had no special significance if a nameless lady passenger on that train had kept her own counsel. Instead, she gave Daeida a word which, in its final application, was to color and influence the lives of millions of people the world over.

What she said was "Hollywood"—the name she had created for her own country estate in Illinois because the property was completely surrounded by holly trees.

Daeida cared nothing about holly. She loved the name. Upon returning to her new Victorian mansion amid the fig trees, she christened

Arrogant Tiburcio Vasquez, Hollywood's most romantic bandit and undisputed outlaw king of California for 23½ years, coupled lightning-fast strikes with careful planning, disappearing immediately into Nichols or Laurel canyons, or hiding out at Greek George's ranch house in the West Hollywood sector of Rancho La Brea. Before robbing a sheep-rancher, for example, he and his men were not above disguising themselves as shearers applying for work. Once hired, they collected a day's pay, gained familiarity with the layout and left, returning later to take the herd with them. Gallantly attentive to the ladies wherever he made an appearance, his charm was so pervasive that after he was finally captured in Hollywood and imprisoned in the Los Angeles City Jail, the sheriff was obliged to issue a public directive forbidding the women of the community to deliver any more flowers or food-delicacies to the prisoner; his cell was already overflowing.

Daeida Hartell Wilcox, born in Hicksville, Ohio, in 1862, was scarcely out of her teens when she married H.H. Wilcox, a middle-aged real estate developer from Topeka, Kansas, who brought her to California in 1883. When, in 1885, he invested in a fig ranch on a 120-acre parcel of land in the northwest sector of Los Angeles, Daeida christened it Hollywood, a name she had adopted from a country estate in Illinois. Six years later, upon the death of her husband, Daeida inherited Hollywood and in 1894 married Philo J. Beveridge.

H. H. Wilcox, whose first two initials have been variously interpreted as "Horace" and as "Harvey" Henderson was born, nonetheless, in Michigan in 1832, thirty years before the birth of Daeida Hartell, the girl who was to become his second wife. A paraplegic from the age of sixteen, Wilcox more than compensated for any physical handicap by a powerful drive to be successful at anything he undertook. He built more than one fortune in real estate development in both Ohio and Kansas and added political accomplishment to his other achievements. In Kansas, three years after his first wife died, he married Daeida and brought her to California where, together, they established Hollywood.

the whole 120-acre parcel "Hollywood."

Although Harvey Wilcox may have suggested "Figwood" as more appropriate, he nonetheless dipped a brush into a can of white paint and painstakingly handlettered the word "HOLLYWOOD" on the gatepost at the entrance to the rancho where Hollywood and Cahuenga boulevards intersect today.

The year 1886 faded into 1887. H.H. Wilcox subdivided his Hollywood tract and filed the map with the county recorder, each street in the rectangular grid set out to be lined with pepper trees.

Sales accelerated. Then, toward the end of the year, the boom collapsed. The Wilcoxes retrenched, giving up their Los Angeles town house in favor of year-round residence in Hollywood, where Harvey Wilcox occupied his time planting pepper trees and making repeated efforts to grow hedges of holly around the house. Despite an inordinate amount of tender loving care the hardiest species of imported English holly refused to take root.

What was worse, even a local variety of red-berried plant, which grew wild almost everywhere else on the outskirts of Los Angeles, wilted

U.S. Senator Cornelius Cole, here with daughter Eleanor, was formidable and famous in "Belle Epoque" Hollywood. But his force is with modern movietown mainly in the place names he left: Cole Street, Seward Street (for his son Seward), Vine Street (because the street plowed through the senator's vineyard), Waring Avenue (for Cole's son-in-law Captain Howard Waring), El Centro (because it was the center of the Cole Ranch), and the legendary Sunset Boulevard because the rut road started on the Cole hill from which the Pacific sunset could be seen.

Nathan Cole, Jr., another Cole entirely, posed for a downtown Los Angeles portraitist in 1880—dressed in the tails he had worn to dedicate the first issue of the Los Angeles Times. A liberal, Cole might have changed the face of both Hollywood and Los Angeles had he retained control of the paper which went broke a month after its founding. The paper went into receivership and then into the hands of the Chandlers. The rest, as they say, is history.

Lillian Gish, D.W. Griffith, and Douglas Fairbanks weren't welcome in the sedate dining rooms of the Lookout Mountain Inn, a conservative restaurant that dished up fried chicken and Parker House rolls—a meal that was apparently worth the forty-five-minute drive on a narrow, rutted road up the hill from Sunset Boulevard.

Laurel Canyon's Trackless Trolley, a product of a short-lived Laurel Canyon Utilities Company, was founded in 1909 and flourished briefly. On a good day, cars could accommodate ten passengers at a time, whisking them at a profitable dime a piece on a one-way trip uphill from Sunset Boulevard to Lookout Mountain Avenue. By 1915, the clumsy trolleys had been replaced by Stanley Steamer buses, but even they were retired a few years later, never to serve again. Meanwhile, the canyon itself became the mountain hideaway for a growing number of "photoplayers," including Bessie Love, who lived at the top of Lookout Mountain.

Hollywood retained some of its original wild-west quality after the turn of the century, despite the proliferation of subdivisions which were rapidly obliterating even the boundaries of the old farms and ranches. In West Hollywood, where Eugene Plummer's ranch house included this extraordinary billiard room for the pleasure of his friends, the forty-acre ranch itself just northeast of Gardner Street and Santa Monica Boulevard was one of the last to undergo subdivision.

and died in Hollywood, while fig and pepper trees flourished.

Although the stream of landbuyers had slowed to a trickle all over the area, Hollywood lots continued to sell little by little, despite the no-holds barred efforts of competitors to divert the flow of investors and migrants away from Hollywood, closer to Los Angeles and south of it.

Among the most formidable of these competitors was U.S. Senator Cornelius Cole who had arrived in Los Angeles in 1881 to take possession of the 483 acres he had accepted in lieu of legal fees for his part in concluding the landgrab efforts of John and Henry Hancock. The Hancocks had fought long and hard to gain control of most of the old Rancho La Brea, one of the earliest Spanish land grants. Ironically, they were broke when they won the case.

Cole, however, wasted no time in settling in on his prize, quickly putting it through subdivision as "Colegrove," coincidentally his wife's maiden name. Then, partially as a public service, he capitalized on his political connections and established the Colegrove Post Office for the delivery of mail to the entire Cahuenga Valley, including Hollywood, which lay adjacent to his property, but north of it.

Senator Cole must have been fully aware of the relationship between Greek George, a government-imported camel herder, and Han-

Hollywood High School was the pride and joy of ultraconservative parents. The cornerstone was laid in 1904 and this photo was taken in 1916. By the mid-fifties, malt shops across the street were a showcase for Carol Burnett, rock king Phil Spector, and Lana Turner, who met a talent agent in the Top Hat Malt Shop—not at Schwab's Drugstore as legend says.

There were mighty changes here from 1901, when this photo of Highland Avenue and Sunset Boulevard was taken, until 1905, two years after Hollywood had become a city, when Hollywood Union High School was completed on the same site.

cock's efforts to deliver mail by "Dromedary Express," although he may not have realized that both George and the camel population in the Hollywood-Colegrove area owed their presence to an error in judgment on the part of the federal government.

In 1858 Congress appropriated $30,000 for the purchase of camels and dromedaries for military purposes, largely due to the insistence of Jefferson Davis, then secretary of war. The whole venture ended in disaster.

As long as they had the animals, however, they had to be corralled. It was Greek George who persuaded Captain Henry Hancock to let him stable them near a wood-and-adobe ranch house on the northern edge of Rancho La Brea, at about where Franklin Avenue and King's Road in Hollywood intersect today.

In the early 1870s, after Greek George had been reduced to tending horses and cattle for the Hancocks, Tiburcio Vasquez, California's most audacious bandit, appeared at the ranch house and demanded shelter. For the next four years, Greek George obliged, while Vasquez terrorized the Americanos throughout Southern California.

For twenty-three and a half years, from the age of 15, Vasquez and his ever-changing band of followers had conducted highly-successful raids on the travelers and ranchers from the northernmost reaches of the state to San Diego without ever being caught. Joaquin Murietta, whose spectacular exploits and brutal forays had made him California's most celebrated highwayman, had survived only three years

Hollywood's Pass School on Sunset Boulevard near Gordon Street served as election headquarters on November 14, 1903, ending the community's hard-fought battle for cityhood. Polls opened at 6 a.m. and closed at 5 p.m. The entire adult male population of 177 showed up and voted, although 12 passed over the cityhood issue. When the ballots were counted, Hollywood had attained the status of Sixth Class City by a narrow 11-vote margin (88 for, 77 against.)

of crime before he was captured and beheaded.

Vasquez, on the other hand, had made a lifelong career of hit-and-run cattle rustling, horse stealing, and burglary, always with a kind of Robin Hood quality which made allies of the Mexicans and Indians who were still trying to wrest a living out of what remained of their once prosperous farms and grazing lands. Time after time, these people protected him from posses.

But his luck ran out at Rancho La Brea in 1874. When the price on his head had reached $15,000, Greek George betrayed him.

Aware of Vasquez's weakness for pretty young ladies and reasonably sure that almost no one in the valley would recognize the bandit on sight, on a pleasant spring evening in May 1874 George persuaded the dapper outlaw to attend a community dance in nearby Nichols Canyon.

Then, when Vasquez had disappeared from sight on his handsome white horse, George saddled his own cow pony and set off posthaste for El Pueblo Grande to tell Sheriff Rowland that the bandit was in the area and was likely to stay nearby.

A few days later, on May 15, at 1 a.m., a hand-picked posse converged at Jones's Corral on Spring Street. This intrepid group departed on horseback at full gallop, following a route along the hills westward toward their canyon destination.

About 4 a.m., having arrived at the foot of the canyon in a dense fog which completely obscured the road uphill, they settled in on a ledge which should have provided a clear view of Greek George's ranch house, and waited.

Late in the morning, the fog lifted. Below them, George's adobe house was clearly visible. Tethered to a tree which shadowed George's kitchen window was Vasquez's white horse, its silver trappings glittering in the sun.

In bright daylight, it was obviously impossible for a posse on horseback to sneak up on the house below without alerting Vasquez. That dilemma was resolved when a wagon came clattering down the canyon road, its two young Mexican drivers heading home after their weekly delivery of firewood. The posse commandeered the wagon and, crowding together under the tarpaulin in back normally used to cover the cargo, they ordered the boys to proceed directly to the adobe house below.

About a hundred yards from the farmhouse, the men leaped from the wagon, guns in hand, and scattered. Harris, Rodgers, and Johnson covered the north side of the house; Hartley and Beers targeted in on the west.

The kitchen door was slightly ajar. Through it Detective Harris could see Vasquez at breakfast, a pretty young girl standing at his side. Harris, followed by the others, made a dash for the partially-opened door, rifle in hand.

Startled by the noise, the girl tried to slam the door, but was stopped by the barrel of Harris's gun. At that moment, Vasquez leaped through the window. He was running like a deer for his horse when Harris shot, the bullet catching Vasquez in the shoulder. At the sound of the first shot, the other officers fired, peppering the bandit with buckshot. He dropped in his tracks.

However, since none of the men had ever knowingly seen Tiburcio Vasquez, there was some question as to the identity of this wounded man.

Initially, he insisted that his name was Alessandro Martinez, an obvious pseudonym, but after some persistent persuasion, the posse elicited the answer they were looking for. This man was, indeed, the outlaw Vasquez.

Rendered docile by pain and convinced that death was imminent, the bandit insisted upon having his last bequests put in writing. Since he could not write, they obliged him.

At the same time, he continued to protest that he had "never killed any human being." It was possible, of course, that the same could not be said for his trusted lieutenant, Clovdovis Chavez, whom he named as the real perpetrator of a series of murders committed in Vasquez's name.

Vasquez was then hoisted into the borrowed wagon and trundled eastward toward the jailhouse along a road already lined with people straining to catch a glimpse of the famous outlaw.

At the jail, the wounded man pleaded to have his irons loosened or removed since he was innocent, and dying anyway. But J.P. Widney, county physician, turned a deaf ear. As the doctor had suspected, Vasquez did not die of his wounds, although his recovery was slow.

Meanwhile, his cell was so constantly filled with flowers, food, and get-well wishes from the women of the community—Indian, Mexican, and American—that the sheriff was forced to issue an edict forbidding any further gifts of admiration to the romantic *bandido*.

Sadly, when Vasquez was finally deemed well enough to travel, he was removed to San Jose where, still protesting that he was being tried for a crime he did not commit, he was convicted of murder and hanged by the neck until dead in March 1875.

Tiburcio Vasquez may have been the first major criminal to live in Hollywood. Regrettably, he was not the last.

In the relative peace and quiet of a fig ranch in the years that followed, only rarely did occasional oldtimers refer back to the days of camel herders and bandits. The subject may have come up again, however, when word got out that Greek George had left the area, moving south, to Whittier.

Naming himself George Allen, he had become an American citizen and is believed to have died in 1915 of natural causes. Nobody ever really knew whether he collected the $15,000 reward for the capture of his almost-friend, Tiburcio Vasquez. But he does appear to have survived quite comfortably for a long time afterwards, without any visible means of support. One conjecture is as good as another.

Toward the end of 1888, the land boom bubble burst. Then, as though that were not enough, the sun burned mercilessly, shriveling the

On Sunset Boulevard, George Knarr was the "Proprieta" of a
livery stable which not only cared for the horses and carriages of
Hollywood's more affluent residents, but rented horses and
wagons to tourists as needed. Proof of the success of Knarr's
venture was visible, even on the darkest night, in the Sunset
Livery sign atop the building, the first electric sign in Hollywood
and environs.

Taking your sweetheart out in the surrey was a reality on
the Sunset Boulevard of 1909 where surreys raced the
Sunday morning trolley from far away Los Angeles. Fifty
years later artists at Twentieth Century-Fox would spend
$2 million to recreate this same scene for Rodger's and
Hammerstein's Oklahoma.

surface of the earth. No rains fell. Wells went dry. The Wilcoxes survived
no better than anybody else, despite their wealth. They, too, gathered
melons, the greener the better, cracking them open and packing the
broken pieces down around the base of young trees, hoping the delicate
roots would draw moisture enough to survive.

Daeida Wilcox also faced up to a bumper crop of figs. Without
a quick and profitable market to turn to before they rotted, she put the
sun to work, drying the figs to preserve their edibility. The experiments
paid off. She not only generated a welcome source of additional income,
she had also created a delicacy which was to become a California
industry.

Suddenly the Wilcoxes were plunged into a changing world.
Public transportation became a problem. Without it, community growth
was impossible. However, even when Harvey Wilcox persuaded the Cahuenga Valley Railway to extend its "dummy" line up Western Avenue
and out on Hollywood Boulevard results were only minimal.

Ironically, it was Senator Cole who profited most from this re-
routing. Before the railcar could reach the end of the line in Hollywood,
Cole's people moved in on Wilcox's prospects at a way-stop and auc-
tioned off large sections of Colegrove instead.

Wilcox had triumphed over setbacks before. He may even have
been prepared for the increasing drop-off in public interest which forced
the railroad to suspend its Hollywood run.

For example, in the first flush of procuring the "dummy" line,
Wilcox negotiated the sale of three sixty-five-foot lots on the southwest

The eccentricities of the movie world eventually made Hollywood infamous, but Paul De Longpré, an internationally famous watercolorist, was the first true eccentric.

This, the living room of his bungalow in the Cahuenga Valley, was decorated with a half million dollars worth of Oriental and American Indian rugs.

This hodgepodge of railroad buildings became the first studio in Hollywood, on the first day of the year, 1909—but it was only because of spite. It started when a Frenchman named René Blondeau trucked the buildings in to open a saloon right after the turn of the century. The indestructible Daeida Wilcox went door to door gathering votes for prohibition. So Blondeau went her one better. The only thing Daeida hated worse than booze was movie people. Thus, Frenchy sold his lot to the Centaur Film Company of New Jersey.

(Above)
Hollywood's first studio was this Victorian-Moorish art gallery and temporary residence of flower-painter Paul De Longpré who, in 1901, having graciously accepted the land as a gift from Mrs. Philo (Daeida Wilcox) Beveridge, built his studio on three sixty-five-foot lots on Cahuenga Boulevard, just north of the Beveridge home on the corner of Prospect (Hollywood Boulevard).

(Left)
If Hollywood ever had any pretensions about its worldwide glory, this oily wreck of a building brought them back to earth. Preserved in its original unique condition on the Paramount Pictures lot, the building (always called the De Mille barn for its first user C.B. De Mille, who filmed The Squaw Man there), is now (1980) slated for status as a national historic shrine. "Which is incredible when you think of the wonderful buildings the studios tore down over the decades," said Agnes De Mille, C.B.'s niece.

43

With egret feathers flying and hobble skirt choking her ankles, silent star Mabel Normand arrives at the Hollywood Hotel with her dog Mack (as in Sennett) for afternoon tea. Inside, a permanent gold star over her table (with the name Mabel in platinum) hovered as a monument of star status. But Mabel Normand became the first in a long line to learn the price of Hollywood fame—a cup of unhappiness. (She died alone after her career simply evaporated in the early twenties.)

Believe it or not, this two pounds of feathers, sixteen ounces of brocade, and terrible fistful of gauze was pretty daring in 1912. But more important, it's one of the first glamour stills to be mailed en masse from Hollywood. The star is Valaska Suratt, an actress who flirted with fame for two decades. Here Miss Suratt is apparently trying to appear as the spitting image of 1912 star Geraldine Farrar. Later she would ape Mary Pickford, Lillian Gish, and Theda Bara. But none of it worked.

Carrie Jacobs Bond, a true Southern lady, ironically became the first to capitalize on Hollywood by writing a bouquet of popular songs from her suite in the Hollywood Hotel. And, though some may blanch at the trite quality of her melodies, nobody can deny their clinging immortality—"A Perfect Day," "I Love You Truly," and "Just A Wearyin' For You."

corner of Hollywood and Cahuenga boulevards to Horace D. Sackett at a substantial reduction in the $3,000 asking price. There was one proviso, however: the buyer must agree to construct a commercial building when the rail line reached Wilcox Avenue, the heart of Hollywood.

Sackett fulfilled his part of the bargain. He constructed Hollywood's first hotel, complete with lobby and parlor, with stairs which led to eighteen bedrooms and one bath. Behind the structure, he provided a barn and corral for his guests—and a vegetable garden for the hotel's culinary department.

In the midst of a critically bad drought, E.C. Hurd and G.C. Baker, two successful miners from Colorado who had also been wholesale and retail distributors of farm implements, were attracted to Hollywood. In short order they bought Wilcox land individually and then shared ownership of the square block between Yucca Street and Sunset Boulevard and Wilcox Avenue and Whitley Avenue, adjacent to the property the Wilcoxes had reserved for themselves.

Perhaps for personal reasons, Harvey and Daeida had added a few full-bearing lemon trees to the fig ranch. Hurd and Baker were so impressed, they planted orchards of lemons on their new land, thus producing the first major citrus crop in the Cahuenga Valley.

To guarantee their farming venture, they invested heavily in a search for adequate water, finally creating a tunnel and reservoir in Brush Canyon to augment a dwindling supply from deep wells scattered throughout the area.

Then, although the population of Hollywood continued to increase at a relatively steady rate, the real estate business had come to a virtual halt. Land-poor, discouraged, and in ill health, in 1891 Harvey Henderson Wilcox, age fifty-nine, died, leaving his worldly goods—all of Hollywood—to his beloved wife, Daeida Hartell Wilcox, age twenty-nine.

Newly-widowed and alone, Daeida assuaged her grief by boarding a train bound for Kansas. Somewhere along the line, she met forty-one-year-old Philo Judson Beveridge, son of former governor of Illinois, John L. Beveridge, and a budding investment expert whose career thus far had included serving the Central Pacific Railroad as an assistant auditor and working as a note broker in his father's banking firm.

Separated from a previous wife and the father of two daughters, Beveridge nonetheless followed Daeida to Hollywood in 1893. In 1894 they were married. Daeida's life took a sudden turn for the better.

In addition to producing four daughters, only two of whom lived to adulthood, Daeida was now able to enter the growing social and political mainstream of the community she had been so instrumental in starting. Large homes had begun to dot the landscape. Local rail lines were regularly carrying passengers from downtown Los Angeles to Hollywood, Sherman (now West Hollywood), and the beaches.

Churchs, banks, schools, and newspapers were beginning to appear. At last, in 1897, the little village of Hollywood acquired its first official Post Office, located in Sackett's Hotel at the corner of Hollywood and Cahuenga boulevards. Daeida Wilcox Beveridge's proprietary in-

Dorothy Davenport with her kitten (it lived in her dressing room) photographed on the set of Our Lady of the Pearls, 1912. Her brave fight against husband Reid's tragic drug addiction made her the model for the character in A Star Is Born. After Wally died in 1923, she financed a film about addiction called Human Wreckage. And when she appeared at a Hollywood awards banquet—broadcast on radio— she proudly announced: "Hello everybody, this is Mrs. Wallace Reid." Virtue, even in Hollywood, pays. She went on to thirty years of successful film writing, dying in the Motion Picture Country Home in 1978. Her last co-authored script, a zany comedy called The Ghost of Drury Lane, is slated for production. Quite a lady, quite a career!

Geraldine Farrar, Hollywood's first "imported star." Cecil B. De Mille lured her from the Metropolitan Opera—where she had been a sensation since she was nineteen. And C.B. started her in all-too-silent versions of her operas Carmen and Joan the Woman. Here, she's decked out in feathers and papier-mâché mail for The Woman God Forgot, which was really a vehicle for early-day superstar Wally Reid.

The Magic Castle (now a chic private club for magicians) started out quite simply as the Holly Chateau—the home of Rollin B. Lane on Franklin Avenue. Here it's under construction in 1909—a lone stand of elegance in a dusty neighborhood. The hills just above the Lane mansion would later become the famous Yamashiro.

terest in directing the history of Hollywood may have had something to do with the resignation of a Mr. Matthews, the first postmaster, in favor of P.J. Beveridge, who quickly replaced him.

As the population grew, ardent residents began to clamor for the status that Hollywood's incorporation as a city would create. Further, the people were demanding control of their own taxes, their own roads, schools, police, and all the other benefits of self-rule.

The movement snowballed until, on November 14, 1903, the polls opened in the Pass Schoolhouse at 6 a.m. and closed at 5 p.m. Every registered adult male in the village (177 in all) cast his vote. When the results were tallied, the village of Hollywood had become a city by a margin of eleven votes!

Even in 1903 there must have been something magical about the name. Certainly there was very little logic behind the hoopla which in a scant sixteen years could catapult this misnamed fruit ranch into the status of a Sixth Class City. Nonetheless, it was officially incorporated as "The City of Hollywood," in "a sector of Los Angeles County containing not less than 500 nor more than 3,000 persons" in a geographic area roughly confined to about twenty-four square miles.

However, while a marginal half of its existing 1,500 citizens rejoiced in Hollywood's emergence as a city, Philo J. and Daeida (Wilcox) Beveridge were not among them. Neither was Philo's father, John L.

Beveridge, who had followed his son to Hollywood and entrenched himself as a political leader of the conservatives in this new frontier.

Another active holdout was H.D. Sackett, whose political leanings may have been influenced by more personal considerations. After all, as the owner of Hollywood's first hotel, he had been free to serve the best interests of the surrounding community as he saw them, without the slightest threat of competition. It was evident that with the advent of city regulations some form of interference was inevitable.

On the other hand, there was Sanford Rich, a proponent of cityhood from Indiana, who had made a fortune as an executive of Swift Meat Packing Company and had "retired" to California. Here, he had made a second fortune as a real estate developer in the northern sector of Hollywood. He had also helped organize Hollywood's first Board of Trade. By accident or design, it wasn't long before he had been "elected" Hollywood's first mayor. In that historic position, he created the city of Hollywood's first, and probably only, motto: "Harmony and Economy." Under the circumstances, there was obviously no room for argument.

Shortly thereafter, the new Board of Trustees named the poinsettia as Hollywood's official flower, a curious choice, in view of the abundance of year-round blossoms which flourished in the formal and informal gardens of such floral-luminaries as Paul De Longpré, Hollywood's first glamorous artist.

Paul De Longpré was a flower-painter. Whatever his talents as an artist, he could never be faulted for his lack of appreciation of care-

If this Oriental palazzo looks familiar, it's because you've seen it many times on the screen—as a background for Marlon Brando in Sayonara, *in the opening frames of* Teahouse of the August Moon, *and in more than a hundred television shows. And it looks real because it is: the walls came from Japan, the murals once belonged to the French royal family. The leading New York importers of Oriental goods, Adolph and Eugene Bernheimer, literally transported their own collection to the Japanese palace in 1914—a mansion that had been under construction for five*

(Continued on page 51)

48

fully cultivated social status as the key to fame and fortune.

A native of Lyons, France, who had been educated in Paris, De Longpré was eking out a dubious living at age twelve by painting flowers on French ladies' fans. At nineteen, he had married a French beauty. Three years later, he sold an oil painting to the Paris Salon and, at thirty-five, wiped out financially by the failure of a French bank, the artist packed up his belongings, his wife, and his two daughters and set sail for New York to make his fortune.

Despite the publicity about America as the great land of opportunity before the turn of the century, the De Longprés found life difficult in New York and flower-models hard to come by during the harsh winters in Manhattan.

With nothing much left to lose, once more Paul De Longpré packed up his family, this time entraining for Los Angeles, where at least the weather was mild and flowers were plentiful. Once settled in Los Angeles, he bought a bicycle and with the tools of his artistry strapped to the rack behind him, De Longpré set out on a half-day's bicycle ride toward Hollywood, where flower-models were sure to be plentiful.

At the corner of Prospect Avenue and Gower Street, De Longpré stopped off at René Blondeau's saloon for a refreshing glass of wine and a sample of the retired perfume importer's French cuisine.

It is only logical to assume that he discussed his problems with this friendly fellow-countryman. In any event, the artist learned pretty quickly that Blondeau knew the most influential social leaders in Hollywood, including Daeida Wilcox, the recent bride of Philo J. Beveridge, another budding leader in community affairs.

If, as Blondeau probably suggested, Paul De Longpré were to invite Mrs. Beveridge to an invitational exhibit of his latest work of art, it was entirely possible that his future as a Hollywood painter of note might be assured.

De Longpré wasted no time in staking his meagre savings on just such an exhibit—and won. He had even told Mrs. Beveridge how he yearned to build an elaborate home in Hollywood. Daeida offered him a deal. If he were serious about building an art studio and Moorish mansion, she would contribute three sixty-five-foot lots facing east on Cahuenga Boulevard, north of the corner of Hollywood Boulevard, to the project. De Longpré leaped at the offer. However, once the studio was completed De Longpré realized that the garden area was much too small. The addition of the corner lot next door would precisely fill his needs.

It must have required more than an impulsive acquiescence for Daeida to have relinquished this corner property. For one thing, she lived there. That's where she'd built her own home and it would be an inconvenience, to say the least, to move farther north, to the corner of Yucca Street, and take the house with her.

Nevertheless, that's exactly what she did. Although she had at first insisted upon payment of $3,000 for the lot alone, she did agree to charge nothing for moving the house.

De Longpré countered, offering her three of what he deemed

his most important original oil paintings, in lieu of cash. Deeply touched by his generosity, Daeida Beveridge relocated the Beveridge family manse.

The deal, as it turned out, was not as naive as it may have appeared to be. De Longpré was, if nothing else, a remarkably talented promoter. His home and gardens became showplaces. Where else in all of California could one hope to visit an elegant Moorish mansion, partake of French cuisine (upon invitation only), and saunter through acres of formal gardens in the company of a world-famous artist on a sunny Sunday afternoon? Only in Hollywood, of course.

In short, even before Hollywood had become a city, it was already acquiring an international reputation for glamour because a French artist and his wife hosted such lavish parties in his Hollywood studio!

And then, alas, the axe fell. Everything changed.

When Hollywood was only a subdivision, the citizenry somehow

years. Occupying the largest flat-topped hill in Hollywood, the Bernheimers had a 360-degree view that grew more glamorous as the decades passed. After the Crash of '29 the house passed through a succession of owners until it was little more than a shell. Then Tom Glover, Sr., buying the house in 1949, restored it and opened the gardens to the public. It's now a restaurant and is almost hidden from view by the Hollywood skyline.

functioned in relative peace and quiet without a lot of laws to live by. There were no police. No jails. Almost no crime, as a matter of fact.

Drunks got drunk. Churchgoers went to church. That's the way it was supposed to be. Then, suddenly, Hollywood had laws and a grim determination to enforce them. For example, after Hollywood's first municipal election on February 1, 1904, a full set of city ordinances effectively created the community's first crimes.

For one thing, the sale of liquor was prohibited, except by pharmacists on prescription. On March 12, 1904, drunkenness and disorderly conduct were arbitrarily prohibited, along with the keeping of disorderly houses, for which specific punishment was prescribed. Speed limits on city streets were set at twelve miles an hour, except for turning corners, entering an intersection, or leaving one, in which case the limit was six miles per hour. Infraction of this law would result in penalties of from one to a hundred dollars, or imprisonment in the county jail for a period not to exceed fifty days.

51

West Hollywood owes its existence to two things: the partnership of General Moses H. Sherman and Eli P. Clark, a pair of college-bred railway promoters from Arizona, and the defunct Los Angeles County Railway Company's steam line, which they purchased in the 1890s, along with a chunk of franchised land which extended from Hollywood to the Beverly Hills city line. Heart of the sector was this corner of Palm Avenue and Santa Monica Boulevard. The settlement which grew up around the car barns, power house, and shops was called Sherman, in honor of the general. However, after Hollywood lost its independent status in 1910, Sherman became West Hollywood.

But the city did have to make arrangements with the county for the incarceration of "criminals," since it had no such facilities, although on the lot which had been set aside for a city hall, some enterprising citizens had constructed a concrete box, six-by-eight-by-ten feet, with a barred opening and an iron door, for the overnight detention of a lawbreaker. So far as is known, it occasionally served as a holding tank for one drunk, about all it could accommodate.

However rewarding this enactment of prohibiton may have been to the conservatives who engineered it, it did have a negative impact on the social life of the community. De Longpré no longer served champagne at his luxurious parties and, in due course, René Blondeau was forced to close his tavern.

Naturally, churches, clubs, banks, and fraternal service organizations flourished. Bond issues provided funds for the schools the people had fought so hard to get, including a $25,000 allocation for the purchase of land and the authorization to construct a Hollywood High School on the corner of Sunset Boulevard and Highland Avenue.

But not everything went smoothly. The city of Hollywood had

apparently forgotten to provide itself with a source of revenue for street repair and other expenses, forcing the Los Angeles county supervisors to allocate the road tax collected in the area to the new city's trustees for maintenance.

On January 16, 1904, the Hollywood Board of Trade held its first annual banquet in the completed portion of the new Hollywood Hotel where, out of consideration for the prohibitionists, officially no wine was served.

H.J. Whitley, one of the community's most powerful business-men who was scheduled to speak on "Hollywood, Its Past, Present, and Future," missed the meeting completely.

However, City Attorney Young was quoted as stating, "Hollywood can never be a large business center, but it is being more and more recognized as a city of homes." Which just goes to show how accurately a novice city attorney in a Sixth Class City could predict the future of his own community.

Apparently, no city official was idle for more than fifteen minutes during the earliest days of cityhood, for ordinances proliferated like well-fed amoebae, bunches at a time: The carrying of concealed weapons was forbidden, along with more specifc regulations for the use of fire-arms where they did exist in the city. More than 2,000 sheep, goats, or hogs were never to be driven through the city streets at any time, unless accompanied by eight competent men in charge. (This law, obviously, is no longer operative.) The riding of vehicles on sidewalks was arbi-trarily forbidden, although only the estates of H.J. Whitley and P.J. Bev-eridge had sidewalks to begin with. Further, "the operation or mainte-nance of slot machines, card machines, or other mechanical devices in the city of Hollywood, for money or other articles of value, depending on chance or hazard" was prohibited.

Sunset Boulevard was mighty muddy after a rain, even in the vicinity of Gower Street. This photo, according to a letter dated February 27, 1963, signed by Mrs. Louise Blondeau Crum, "looks like me with my little friend Lillian Lepords, taken about 1896, looking east . . . the building on the left is Hollywood's only blacksmith shop . . . and behind the gap in the trees is the Pass School, where there were nine grades in three rooms. . . ." The photo was probably taken as an easterly view from Sunset Boulevard and Gower Street, when Gower was called Romaine.

This could be Main Street, Anytown—1905. With its livery stable, town hall, and cobble streets, Hollywood in 1905 was a dead ringer for Pensacola, Florida, Abilene, Texas, or Bangor, Maine. Vaudeville played here—but only on Thursdays, and then in the church social hall. Show people were not encouraged to stay long enough to unpack their suitcases.

Glamorous Hollywood as Mr. and Mrs. Horace Henderson Wilcox knew it about 1890. Unfinished house and orchard in the foreground were centered at about where Hollywood and Cahuenga boulevards meet today.

Rich farmers, the A. G. Bartletts, and their ranch spread out as far as the eye could see up into the hills. The grape vineyards in the foreground would wither and die in today's smog. And that's just what many of the vineyards did. But Bartlett might get some consolation from the fact that his land today would bring a cool $20 million.

Nonetheless, in its first year of existence, investors in the city of Hollywood had spent more than $800,000 in the construction of 144 new buildings within its limits, including $100,000 for the new Hollywood Hotel and the $12,000 Mrs. Beveridge had invested in construction of the Wilcox Building on the southeast corner of Hollywood and Cahuenga boulevards.

By accident or intent, Daeida's new building was to have a catalytic effect on the future of Hollywood. A spacious banking room dominated the corner space on the first floor. Adjacent to it, on the Prospect Avenue (Hollywood Boulevard) side was a modern drugstore, a genuine innovation. On the Cahuenga Boulevard side, two store rooms awaited tenants.

Upstairs, however, the building provided a large dance floor with rostrum; a billiard and card room; an office; and an area for dispensing soft drinks and cigars. It was here that E.W. Elliott, a retired Chicago druggist, and his wife started the Hollywood Club, with bimonthly dances. And it was here that Hollywood launched its first theatre—for amateur theatricals, of course.

However, it was Paul De Longpré who emerged as the first president of the Hollywood Club, with Elliott, the founding father, serving as secretary-manager.

Then, on June 24, 1905, Daeida's basic motive for construction of the Wilcox Building became eminently clear with the formal opening of Hollywood National Bank, representing investments from fifty-six stockholders, with only seventy shares held by the directors.

The frontier charm of Hollywood was fading fast. On November 16, 1907, Hollywood's first census report was filed. Population had increased to 3,415; 835 residents were under sixteen years of age, 2,580 were over; 615 owned homes, 239 rented them.

From its very onset, Hollywood had defied rational explanation, and no wonder. If the first census were to be any indication of the pattern of its growth, how could future industries hope to find a common denominator among an ethnic mix which included 103 immigrants from England, 102 from Germany, 86 from Canada, 20 from France, 28 from Ireland, 24 from Scotland, and representative residents from 25 other countries.

Of American migrants who had chosen to settle in Hollywood, 634 were from elsewhere in California, 277 came from Illinois, 176 from Ohio, 67 from Iowa, 158 from New York, 90 from Michigan, 158 from Pennsylvania, 135 from Missouri, 135 from Indiana, 63 from Wisconsin, and 47 from Minnesota.

By the fall of 1909 the burdens of running a city had mounted until the early enthusiasm for "Harmony and Economy" as a motto had become a mockery. On December 22, Ordinance 425 was passed, providing for an election to determine whether the city of Hollywood should consolidate with the city of Los Angeles under the Los Angeles charter.

A week later, on the 29th, Ordinance 426 required that free dogs be muzzled. There was probably no connection. However, on January 5, 1910, Ordinance 440, another non sequitur, changed the name of Prospect Avenue officially to Hollywood Boulevard.

Of far greater significance was an apparently inconsequential suit filed in 1907 by a group of Los Angeles citizens who demanded $500,000 in damages from the city for failing to furnish water to certain parts of its area while selling water outside the territory.

This hassle had begun long ago, during the early history of the Pirtle Water Company and the Union Hollywood Water Company, when the city brought action to prevent diversion of water to Hollywood from the river basin. Along about 1903, Hollywood was still talking about annexing the northern part of the Cahuenga Valley to Los Angeles. That

A lovely house in the country! And this home owned by Henry Claussen was the only house in the original Hollywoodland—1905. A rooming house down the street had a sign that read "No dogs and actors allowed!" And the owner meant "movie" actors. Ten years after the Claussen Mansion was finished that family became some of the first signers of a petition to keep the movies and movie people out of Hollywood. They called themselves "The Committee of Conscientious Citizens." They lost of course, but only barely.

move was vigorously opposed by the water board because of the burden it promised to place on available water supplies.

After Hollywood had become a city, its water engineers had successfully drilled for water at Las Palmas and Franklin avenues, at Selma and Hudson avenues, at Kings Road south of Santa Monica Avenue (now Boulevard), and at the southwest corner of Sunset Boulevard and Western Avenue.

Other wells were put down below the then-city at Jefferson Street, but there was still not enough water to provide for the growth of the city.

In the meantime, however, the city water company made a deal: the West Los Angeles water company would be allowed to pump 200,000 gallons of San Fernando water into the Hollywood reservoir if it would in turn pump an equal amount into the city mains from its Jefferson Street wells. The $500,000 suit included an injunction against further replacing good San Fernando water with questionable Jefferson Street water.

The same year, William Mulholland, a water engineer, and some associates of the Los Angeles city water system, promised to deliver water from the Owens Valley 250 miles away to the San Fernando Valley reservoir by 1913 for only $24.5 million. Los Angeles sponsored two elections to gain approval for the necessary bonds—and work was started in 1908.

All through the next year, the people of Hollywood talked about plenty of water. Even Hollywood's city fathers were convinced that annexation to the city of Los Angeles was the only possible solution to an imminent dilemma. Election was held in February of 1910. There was no contest.

The city of Hollywood was dead. Zap! Harmony, economy, and the poinsettia were reduced to a mere "northwest sector of the city of Los Angeles."

But there was a bright note. At least some of its city ordinances had died with it, such as prohibition. Too late, unfortunately, to save René Blondeau's tavern.

On the other hand, nothing is all bad. Late in September of 1910, Blondeau's tavern and barn were put to a different kind of use, a much

(Above)
Water comes to Hollywood. But the price meant a severe loss of identity and control for the city which joined Los Angeles under protest. The store, windmill, and post office in the distance were at the crossroads of what would become Edgemont Street and Fountain Avenue—a busy Hollywood intersection.

(Opposite)
Oil, booze, and movies had all come to Hollywood when a London photographer took this panorama of the basin. The Britisher set up his camera at the hill at the top of Orange Street looking south to Sunset Boulevard and the oil derricks of what is now the Wilshire Boulevard District—an area slated to be called the Miracle Mile in the 1930s. "It was paradise in those days," said Lillian Gish—who took the train out in the spring of 1912 when this picture was taken. "I came West for a picture not because of a trend but because I'd been sick. And when the train headed into the outskirts of Hollywood, you could smell orange blossoms, roses, and jasmine. We thought it was paradise."

more profitable one in fact, and considerably more long range.

A Mr. David Horsley, president of the Nestor Film Company, Staten Island, New York, and a Mr. Al Christie, a movie director, arrived in Hollywood and, on their second day in town, leased the whole northwest corner of Sunset Boulevard and Gower Street from Mrs. Blondeau, widow of the late René Blondeau, former French tavern owner.

Two months later, the Nestor Company staffed Hollywood's first motion picture studio in an abandoned French bistro some distance from downtown Los Angeles. Which is how it came to pass that, international publicity notwithstanding, not one single feature film was ever produced in the city of Hollywood.

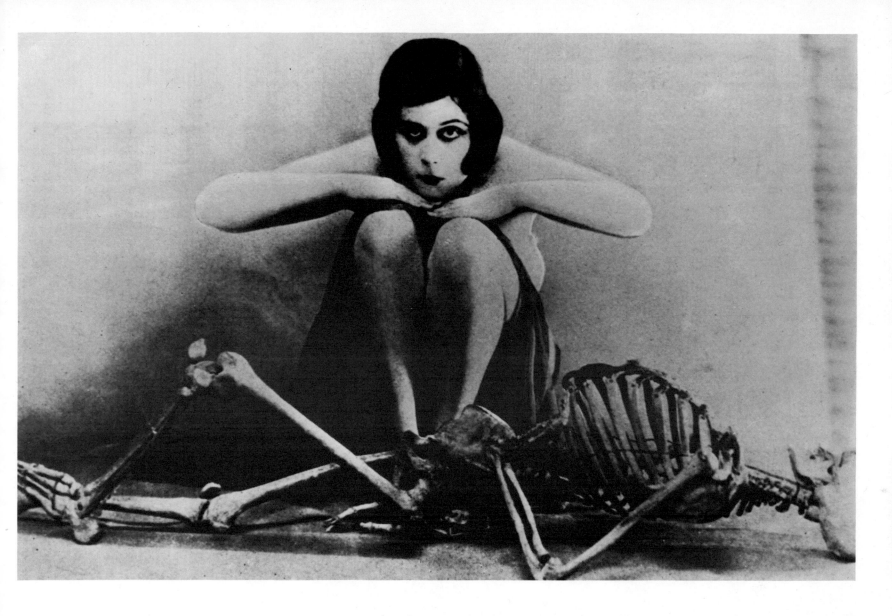

III ESCAPE FROM REALITY, HOLLYWOOD STYLE
1911 to 1922

Theda Bara, vamping over the bones of a "victim of love," 1916. Her name was actually Theodosia Goodman, the daughter of a Cincinnati tailor.

One block west of Grauman's Chinese, the elegant Garden Court Apartments, now a shabby relic, in 1935 featured two private ballrooms, tennis courts, and sumptuous suites for rich and famous movie people, but only after the original arbitrary ban on renting to "theatrical trash" had been lifted.

Like the traditions of monarchy wherein the king is dead, long live the king, the City of Hollywood was dead, but long live Hollywood anyway. And live it did, nurturing itself on the developing science of moving pictures.

Moviemakers had been filming in and around Los Angeles for several years before the Horsleys arrived. American Biograph and Mutoscope Company had been in business since 1906, and D.W. Griffith had been in town for western backgrounds. In 1909 Adam Kessel and Charles Baumann, a pair of names to reckon with, had built the open stage on Alessandro Street which was later to become headquarters for Mack Sennett Keystone Company.

6129

But Hollywood was a slow starter. It took a lot of doing to breathe new life into an isolated California community in October 1911 when all you had to work with was the old Blondeau, tavern on the northwest corner of Sunset Boulevard and Gower Avenue, and some illegal photographic equipment. However, having rented the entire corner and all of its buildings for forty dollars per month, William and David Horsley, New Jersey moviemakers, and Al G. Christie, a director of westerns, established Nestor Moving Picture Company. Furthermore, in the first week of occupancy, the company produced Hollywood's first motion picture, *Her Indian Hero,* with real Indians and a leading lady named Dorothy Davenport, later to become Mrs. Wally (Florence) Reid.

Ostensibly, Southern California was an ideal setting for movie-making. It boasted of sunny mild weather 350 days a year and an un-

The Hollywood Studio Club, organized in 1916 as a home away from home "for young ladies of moderate income, particularly those associated with the motion picture industry," first settled its charges in this large residence at 6129 Carlos Avenue, the former home of a Mrs. E. W. Twist.

(Opposite, top)
On the steps of the Hollywood Studio Club in 1919, pretty girls posed endlessly for promotional photos, hoping against hope for a "break" in pictures. The continuing barrage of publicity throughout the United States fed the influx of glamour-struck movie-aspirants into the Hollywood melting pot.

(Opposite, bottom)
At the Hollywood Studio Club in 1917, not all of these young women were unknown actresses. As a case in point, on the floor in the center of this photo is Mary Pickford, perhaps the brightest star ever to endure in the motion-picture firmament.

limited variety of scenery. Actually, while the weather was predictably better than that of New Jersey, especially in the winter, it was not all that good—and it certainly wasn't the only reason these motion picture pioneers appeared to be streaming as far west as they could go without setting their hats afloat.

For one thing, most of these producers had already infringed on the Edison patents to such a degree they had set a national industrial dispute in motion which came to be known as the Patents War. Further, it was fought like a real war, with violence, and by mercenaries, in a manner of speaking, since the hired sluggers were professional hoods. It was time to be moving along.

Hollywood was strategically located. It was out of the main stream of railway travel and it was close enough to the Mexican border to permit relatively rapid exit from the U.S. should the need arise. As late as May 12, 1912, the wild west lived again on the streets of Hollywood—not all of it on film! That was the month the Nestor Company was taken over by Universal, a voracious combine of moviemakers who intended to absorb Kay-Bee (Kessel and Baumann) as well. But Kay-Bee resisted. Universal's general manager, William Swanson, counterattacked by sending Charles Rosher, a Nestor cameraman, to encourage management to change its mind.

Rosher, armed with power of attorney and a bunch of cowboys packing guns, marched into the studio. Disrupting a card game, he instantly appropriated the files and took control. It was as easy as that.

The movies had brought with them some strange goings-on. At first, the solid citizens of Hollywood, a conservative lot at best, had regarded the influx of moviemakers with tolerant suspicion. In time, however, since these "foreigners" appeared to have their own way of doing things, this suspicion hardened into ill-concealed hostility.

If there was ever a point of no return for Hollywood it happened here at the gates of Hollywoodland, a subdivision with castle towers, Black Forest cottages, and Ruritanian hunting lodges. It also had the best press agent in California history, Harry Chandler of the Los Angeles Times (coincidentally one of Hollywoodland's founders). The Times helped but it was Chandler's idea of a supersign soaring above the hills that turned the tide. It had letters the height of a five-story building and was lit by 4,000 light bulbs. The cost? (It would cost $249,300 to replace sixty years later—sans lights.) The busses, below, were started before the advent of freeways to transport the "8 to 5" people to their jobs and back to the fantasy hills of Hollywoodland.

Hollywood's first major theatrical production, Shakespeare's Julius Caesar, *widely touted locally as "the greatest show on earth," opened May 19, 1916, in what was later to become the Hollywood Bowl. The play starred such New York stage luminaries as Theodore Roberts as Caesar; Tyrone Power (Sr.) as Brutus; Frank Keenan as Marc Antony; William Farnum as Cassius; Douglas Fairbanks as Young Cato. Grace Lord as Cleopatra and Mae Murray as Barbaric Dancer were the last two names listed on the program. Stage set designed by Frank Lloyd Wright, Jr.*

Neighborhoods were restricted and housing became increasingly difficult for the "movies," as the *people* associated with the industry were called. They were barred from the best clubs—and the best neighborhoods—along with Jews and Negroes.

So, they took advantage of the only avenues of social survival left open to them. They built their own neighborhoods, their own subdivisions. They lined their streets with small bungalows. And they took to the hills of Hollywood, where they built castles and mansions which dwarfed Paul De Longpré's Moorish palace to the dimensions of a slightly oversized dollhouse by comparison. They invaded Hollywood Boulevard and built shops, bringing to them the flavor of New York, adding restaurants, apartment buildings, delicatessens. Then, in the heart of Hollywood on Wilton Place, just north of Hollywood Boulevard, they struck a lethal blow at the old guard. They build Hollywood's first synagogue! Finally, since they were *personae non gratae* in some places in Hollywood, studio executives retaliated by closing their own gathering places to outsiders. Sauce for the goose was certainly sauce for the gander.

Daeida Beveridge's dream of perpetuating Hollywood as an ultra-conservative Christian community was doomed. By mid-summer of 1914 she had witnessed the installation of telephones, inside plumbing, electricity, automobiles, oil fields, and the movie industry, all in her own front yard. On August 14, 1914, Daeida Beveridge, Hollywood's first lady,

The thunder of magic roared out of this quaint little street of houses—the Charlie Chaplin Studio (on LaBrea Avenue and now the site of A&M Records). "The Chaplin Studio was like a big toy chest," says Jackie Coogan, who, at four, came onto the lot with his dad to star in the first Chaplin-produced feature, The Kid, 1921. *"He was the only producer on the lot—the studio was ours. Sometimes the camera wouldn't run for ten days while Charlie got an idea." In 1980, film historian Kevin Brownlow reviewed the years at this studio and said, "When you realize how much he put into his work it's no wonder he had problems in his private life."*

A&M Records today.

passed away. With her death, every vestige of the rural community she had helped to create faded from view.

The once-quiet streets of Hollywood had quickly become the best of all possible movie locations. Private homes were "borrowed" as settings for romantic scenes; businesses were "robbed" and "burglarized" for the camera; and Christie's Bathing Beauties, shameless in their form-revealing bathing suits, lunched *in costume* at local cafes between "takes!" Horrors!

Furthermore, this immoral behavior produced shocking reports that "our young ladies are being corrupted by exposure to lipstick and face powder!"

Meanwhile, at risk of life and limb, automobiles, at the hands of handsome leading men like Wally Reid, careened through streets and alleys at breakneck speed, tailgated by another car with camera and cameramen lashed to its hood. A few blocks away, Tom Mix and a posse may have been raising clouds of dust chasing the bad guys over conveniently-adjacent grazing land.

Moviemaking was fun, in those days. And glamorous. It was also destructive, especially for those who found themselves suddenly both rich and famous.

Young, uneducated, and scarred by poverty, many of the early on-camera people were emotionally crippled by success. Whereupon, perhaps to conceal their feelings of inadequacy, they embarked on a lifestyle of flamboyant excesses equaled only by the hedonism of *La*

Thomas Harper Ince (in the McIntosh cap) put an entire Wild West Show on his payroll to serve as a backdrop for his major star, William S. Hart, in the Stetson. These Indians came part and parcel with the show—including their costumes and trained buffalo. This kind of lavish artistic integrity made Ince and his studio, Inceville near Santa Monica, a rival of D.W. Griffith in importance. A former Mary Pickford director, he was so influential that French cineaste Louis Delluc said: "Griffith is cinema's first director, Ince its first prophet."

Queen Elizabeth of Belgium found Hollywood's doors fully open to her on a 1919 visit. But she only wanted one thing—to watch Tom Ince film a William S. Hart western. Here, surrounded by her honor guard, she watches the guys shoot 'em up. But for Ince, tragedy was around the bend. He died of a bleeding ulcer and heart attack on William Randolph Hearst's yacht in 1923— before he realized his full power. As usual in Hollywood his name was quickly trampled under commercialized feet; the Ince runner-up, Irving Thalberg, got the glory.

Dolce Vita. At the same time, they worked hard. Hours were long and what the earliest silents may have lacked in tedium for the performers, they more than made up for in bodily risk.

Even the daintiest actresses ran for their lives over rugged terrain, dropped out of windows, crawled over barbed wire fences, and nearly drowned in the icy Pacific, all for "art's sake"—and big money, after the star system had become entrenched, of course.

Before 1908, everybody associated with moving pictures was nameless, except for being identified with the production company for which he, or she, worked. It was enough to be known as "The Biograph Girl," or "The Girl with the Curls," or "A Mack Sennett Bathing Beauty," until two moviemakers locked horns over a pretty girl named Florence Lawrence, then the most popular Biograph personality.

Apparently she'd been quite happy with her semi-anonymity at Biograph until an upstart named Carl Laemmle decided he wanted her to join his newly-formed Independent Moving Picture Company (IMP). Even her most ardent admirers had never heard of Florence Lawrence until Laemmle himself quietly "leaked" a story to the press to the effect that Florence Lawrence, better known as "The Biograph Girl" had been killed in a streetcar accident in St. Louis.

Shortly thereafter, the same Carl Laemmle, president of Independent Moving Pictures Company, publicly denounced the story, attributing it to the Biograph Company to conceal the fact that the beauteous Miss Lawrence had left her former employer. She would here-

einafter be known as Florence Lawrence, the IMP Girl, a Carl Laemmle star. Naturally, Laemmle offered her more money but by accident or design she never really regained the popularity Biograph had given her. Laemmle dropped her. Finally, after minor acting roles elsewhere and a few demeaning jobs for sheer survival, in 1939 she committed suicide.

Meanwhile, however, every other actor had begun to demand the same kind of personal recognition. The star system had been born, conceived, and nurtured in fabrication. It was only logical that it would spawn its own creative parasite—the motion picture press agent. In pursuit of his duties, it was the ever-present press agent who breathed glamour into an otherwise exploitive business.

Actually, there was nothing very glamorous about the drive and ingenuity of movie producer Carl Laemmle and his fellow production-company executives. Grudging admiration, maybe, but nothing one could actually call glamour.

For example, unhampered by ethical considerations, Carl Laemmle formed Universal Film Company by gobbling up as many small production companies as he could, including Nestor, Hollywood's first moviemaker, and moving the whole package to more than 250 acres of leased ranch land in North Hollywood.

As founding father owning controlling stock, Carl Laemmle became the new company's first president; Patrick Powers was named vice-president, and Nestor's David Horsley was secretary. To be sure that the public was aware of this earthshaking turn of events, Laemmle topped his own best record to date for sheer *chutzpah.* He not only invited the local populace to view Universal City from the inside and provided coach service to and from, but he reported to the national press that, by order of the Secretary of the Navy, the Pacific Coast Fleet would proceed up the Los Angeles River and, upon passing Universal, it would fire a salute of honor beside the new film metropolis!

What makes this story so fascinating is the fact that there was no possible way any part of the U.S. Fleet could have sailed up or down the narrow confines of the Los Angeles River, *if* it had had water in it, which it didn't. What it did have in it, in 1915, was a large water main laid along its river bed.

Meanwhile, back in Hollywood, class distinctions were beginning to make themselves felt in the movie business itself. According to historian Kevin Brownlow, "the lower orders were extras, cowboys, stagehands, and people who worked at Universal." At the top of the ladder, social acceptance was pretty well assured if the movie person

The United Artists sign their corporation papers in 1919—D.W. Griffith, Mary Pickford, Albert Banzhaf, Charles Chaplin, Dennis O'Brien and Douglas Fairbanks. It was a historic but bittersweet occasion—because Griffith, Pickford, Fairbanks and Chaplin had already seen their true glory days. And though United Artists (after adding Walt Disney, Gloria Swanson and Sam Goldwyn) would have annual incomes (grosses) of 25 million, Mickey Mouse became its greatest star and a youngster named David O. Selznick its greatest producer.

The Little Tramp, the girl with the golden curls and stalwart Doug Fairbanks clown in the sunshine of an era when movies were still fun. Chaplin would die an exile from Hollywood, Mary Pickford ended as a recluse in Pickfair and Fairbanks died in his sleep at 55. "We didn't know what we were doing," said Anita Loos. "But we were at the center of the greatest art form the world had ever known—for a while."

D.W. Griffith, the first great director of the movies, and Ben Alexander, 7, the first in a long line of boy stars, on a tramp steamer to France during the filming of "Hearts of the World," (1918) the first war propaganda film. Griffith took Ben, Lillian Gish and other cast members right to the front and then rushed the film back to London for processing. "But the action just didn't look the way Griffith wanted," said Miss Gish. "So he moved back to Hollywood where war behaved the way he wanted."

was obviously rich and/or had been calculating enough to marry a title, rich or poor.

In the wake of the Russian Revolution and World War I, there were more than enough titles to go around—and go around they did. Actress Connie Bennett and actress Gloria Swanson both married the Marquis de Falaise—at different times. On the other hand, there were lavish parties launched in honor of The Princess Beatriz de Ortego y Braganza of Alhambre Granada, Spain, who was later exposed as an out-of-work typist from San Francisco. Film producer Thomas Ince toppled all previous records for social pretension when he escorted the real Elizabeth, Queen of Belgium, through his new studio facility in 1919. (Few of the queens in Hollywood then—and now—were of genuine royal blood.) However, any opportunist with an apparently inexhaustible supply of money could masquerade as a blueblood and, without half trying, attract as fine a set of impoverished aristocracy as anyone might wish.

With the advent of Prohibition, "the crazies" spread through Hollywood like a plague, and every madness of the movie colony was faithfully reported by the press. Pretty young girls and handsome young men elbowed each other out of the way at studio gates, pushing and shoving to be first at even the slightest hint of a "cattle call," when a studio was open to casting extras and other minor roles. Hungry actors, many already costumed in western outfits, clustered hopefully at the corner of Gower Street and Sunset Boulevard in such numbers the corner itself came to be known as Gower Gulch, a name it still holds although the studios are long gone.

Most were strangers to California; few had any kind of theatrical experience. All they had was hope, kept alive by youth and beauty. It was inevitable that the latter two assets should be recognized as marketable by film producers. But not necessarily on film. For some of the girls, whose best performances for an influential studio affiliate may have been on the casting couch, it was a relatively short step to fame and fortune. Others found it both expedient and profitable to stick with the casting couch, so to speak. As a matter of fact, some of the best brothels in Hollywood and Los Angeles were owned and operated *in absentia* of course, by studio executives.

Meanwhile, in the real world of Hollywood, outside the film industry, the secretary of the community's board of trade was so pressured she was elevated to the position of a paid assistant and given space in the office of Philo Beveridge at the northeast corner of Cahuenga and Hollywood boulevards. While wages in the movie industry ranged upwards from an enviable $3 per day for extras to as much as $3,000 per week for "stars"—tax free—secretaries and other menials embarked on more basic pursuits were considered amply rewarded with considerably less.

These were the people who lived vicariously in the flamboyant escapism of the movies. Until the picture business invaded the area, Hollywood had basked in the glory of its churches, of which there were many, its service clubs, banks, and land investments, all neatly tabulated.

This faded news photo looks a little foolish now—a rotogravure dinosaur of Doug Fairbanks and Mary Pickford sending a telegram to Santa Claus in 1922. But it was big stuff then because Doug and Mary, the world's first superstars, would spend the rest of their lives bowing to the roar of the crowd. Mary would go so far as to hide herself away when she started growing old. "My fans would not forgive my growing old in public." She dropped Doug, too. But in 1978 Mary asked her friend Adela Rogers St. Johns: "Will they understand? Was it right?" Adela merely shook her head. "Who else but her would know what it was like to be the first movie star?"

What it lacked, *en toto,* was any form of art or culture. There were no art galleries, no public concerts, no theaters—until 1916 when, on Friday, May 19, a small group of civic organizations startled the community with what was widely proclaimed as "the greatest show on earth." What it really was, in fact, was a semi-professional production of Shakespeare's *Julius Caesar,* scarcely earthshaking in itself. However, it did make history, since it was enacted in the natural canyon amphitheatre which was later to become the world-famous Hollywood Bowl. It was also to provide designer Lloyd Wright, the eminent architect's son, with an opportunity to create the controversial acoustical shell which served as a prototype for the more sophisticated shell which dominates the Bowl today.

In 1917, while World War I's "war to end all wars" accelerated throughout Europe, the ordinary people of Hollywood organized a Community Sing, sold Liberty Bonds, and looked forward to thirty-five nightly performances, live, of Sir Edwin Arnold's *Light of Asia,* starring dancer Ruth St. Denis, and actors Walter Hampton and Ellis Reed.

This esoteric opus, a great success, was staged amid fruit trees in the tropical gardens of Krotona, hilltop retreat and educational center for the local branch of the American Theosophical Society.

Here, incidentally, in the cluster of Spanish and Moorish buildings which housed Krotona members, the society sponsored regular courses for adults in theosophy, philosophy, astrology, psychology, and occult sciences, filling the gap (hopefully) between scientific and theosophical education.

Meanwhile, there was nothing esoteric about moviemaking in the flatlands of Hollywood. As the star-system solidified, "names" became increasingly important to the filmmakers who were, more often than not, also the major profit-takers as distributors and exhibitors. At the same time, the most popular players of the period had begun to realize that they were looked upon as studio "properties" who *belonged* to their employer. As such, since most properties were bought, they certainly deserved to be paid for—in great big, tax-free dollars.

Established veterans like Mary Pickford and Charlie Chaplin were the first to join the ranks of millionaire super-stars. Chaplin did it in 1917, just ahead of Mary Pickford, when he demanded and received more than $1 million from First National for one year's work.

In that year he made four films—all classics, not a bad record for a Cockney street-urchin still in his twenties who had left London in 1913 to tour America with a vaudeville troupe and left the troupe to become a Mack Sennett Keystone comic, all in a single year!

Sennett had signed him for a year at a beginning salary of $130 per week which would increase to $175 three months later. However, after Chaplin's first film, Sennett threatened to fire him, partly because he considered him unfunny and partly because he believed him to be excessively egotistical. This latter quality may have been responsible for Charlie's ultimate success as the "little tramp," since, to overcome Sennett's low opinion of him, he created a ludicrous costume from the wardrobes of fellow workers.

He borrowed Fatty Arbuckle's trousers and hat, Ford Sterling's boots (worn on the wrong feet because they were much too big), a painted mustache filched from a Keystone Kop, a cane from an office coat rack, and a walk adapted from a flatfooted London cabbie he had once known.

The guffaws his outfit elicited as he made his way back to the set convinced him that he'd done something right. Sennett gave him another chance. Truth of the matter is that Chaplin made thirty-five films in one year—including *Tillie's Punctured Romance* with Marie Dressler, a classic if only because it was Hollywood's first full-length comedy feature.

Chaplin's success was assured. At twenty-six, having become the world's highest-paid performer, he was also gaining questionable fame for his passionate pursuit of great riches and very young girls, four of whom he married. Of those he did not marry, only Joan Barry, an aspiring actress in her very early teens, took him to court for his over-sight. It's entirely possible she felt she had good cause. After all, she was pregnant.

As though embroiling him in a paternity suit weren't enough, young Miss Barry added testimony that resulted in an indictment against him for allegedly taking her across state lines for immoral purposes, a charge that was subsequently dropped. The paternity suit was more difficult, despite some inconclusive blood tests. Finally, the jury ordered Chaplin to support the infant, and the matter should have died there.

But Chaplin was not destined to be free of scandal. When, at fifty-four, he announced his intention to marry Oona O'Neill, the eighteen-year-old daughter of American playwright Eugene O'Neill, the world press, bored with the battle scores of World War II, had a field day with Chaplin's past peccadillos.

A radiant Marion is engulfed in this especially assembled panorama of stars for her picture Show People, *1928. Marion is at far right next to William S. Hart. Swanson, Ramon Novarro, and other luminaries create a desperate picture of Hollywood engulfed with sound. Marion would say later that it was like watching ghosts to replay the film. But replay it she did since it earned Hearst's approval for showing at his castle San Simeon.*

Reginald Denny, Norma Shearer, Clifton Webb, and Douglas Fairbanks, Jr., converse on Miss Shearer's MGM sofa in a setside tête-à-tête that is almost too cute to be real. Shearer, protected from the cruel realities of Hollywood by her mogul-boy husband Irving Thalberg, specialized in this type of press. "Let's put it this way," said Crawford about Shearer, "the rest of us work for a living."

Those are real tigers and a near-nude star in this sequence of a dissolute Roman courtesan never used in a De Mille movie. (It was supposed to be a flashback for Manslaughter.) As the film rolls, De Mille moves the camera closer and closer to the woman's feet—finally filling the screen with them. Editors thought nothing of this, De Mille's apparent foot fetish became a trademark in all of his early silents. Claudette Colbert, a major De Mille star, said of her costumes for a Roman-Egyptian epic, "You could have put all my costumes on at once and still not have been protected from a chill on an August night.

Cecil B. De Mille went down in history as "God's personal director" after such epics as King of Kings and The Ten Commandments. But in his lustful early days, De Mille filled his pictures with a gallery of erotica such as this lavish prize fight (from Male and Female). The girls boxing are twins and, in the process of the scene, got off hefty perversities during the body punches. De Mille found a magic formula for sneaking around the censors. De Mille heroines (most often Gloria Swanson) or heroes (most often Wallace Reid) always got punished for their transgressions. But first De Mille showed those scenes on a lavish scale.

Considering her social pressures, it's a wonder Marion got any films in the can. Here with Lindberg, Louis B. Mayer (far right) and Howard Hughes (behind Davies), the star welcomes "Lucky Lindy" to Hollywood with an afternoon tea in her studio bungalow. She had also greeted George Bernard Shaw, Queen Marie of Roumania, and the Prince of Wales. (When Hearst felt MGM was not giving Marion her due, he sawed the bungalow in half and moved it—along with her contract, and his goodwill—over to Warner Brothers.)

Gleefully they rehashed the record of his every marriage from the first, at twenty-nine, to Mildred Harris, sixteen; his second, at thirty-one, to Lita Gray, also sixteen, who stuck around long enough to bear him two sons, Charles, Jr., and Sydney, before she divorced him in 1927. (That divorce was so sensational that women's clubs in many states rose up in horror—and banned Chaplin pictures from their movie houses. The ban, however, was short-lived.)

Chaplin's next marriage was to actress Paulette Goddard, age twenty, whom he married in 1936, after five years of "constant companionship." That marriage too, came a cropper in 1942, midway between Joan Barry's paternity accusations and Chaplin's child-support payments.

Chaplin finally settled down with Oona O'Neill, but not in the U.S. Enough was enough, already. He had made millions in America, although he had never so much as applied for U.S. citizenship, thereby avoiding taxes. He had fought with unions and the IRS. His left-wing political views got him into trouble with the House UnAmerican Activities Committee. He refused their subpoena to testify, and, while he was

The Hollywoodland sign on Mount Lee as seen from Lake Hollywood
in the late 20s. Castillo del Lago, a nine level private residence
of great beauty and charm, is seen in the middleground.

Wolff's Lair, a sprawling castle complex on Durand Drive in the Hollywood hills, is the former home of television star Efrem Zimbalist, Jr., the son of the famous concert-violinist whose name he bears. Superbly maintained, it is now owned by author and realtor, Bob Crane.

The entrance gates to Hollywoodland under construction in 1923.

Mañana, the fox terrier, had a Spanish pedigree half a block long. His owner, Antonio Moreno, could trace his patents of nobility about as far as the steamer from which he docked in New York as a fourteen-year-old immigrant. Here Tony helps publicity cameramen build his identity—facade first. Moreno's name was really Garride Monteagudo, and he came over as a kitchen helper.

No indignity was too low for the Hollywood flacks. Here Moreno, who had a team of gardeners for his Hollywood mansion, mows the lawn while smoking a Havana cigar (he never smoked) and wearing a sombrero (hardly his style).

With his muscles sculpted by a studio masseur, Moreno lounges in a tile-lined pool—also furnished by D.W. Griffith and the studio.

traveling abroad, the attorney general retaliated by confiscating his re-entry visa. Unable to return, Chaplin retreated with his young bride to Switzerland, where he could probably visit his money in person.

The visa was reinstated in the late fifties, but he did not return to the U.S. until 1971 and then only by invitation. In April of that year, a frail little old man, he flew to New York to accept a special honor from the Film Society at Lincoln Center, then on to the Music Center in downtown Los Angeles, about twelve miles from Hollywood and his old studios on Sunset Boulevard and La Brea Avenue. There, since he had never been given an Oscar, the revered Academy of Motion Picture Arts and Sciences finally presented him with a Special Award. He was led to the podium. He smiled. He accepted the plaque. He was led away. The next day he returned to Switzerland.

Maybe it mattered, all that acclaim, all that ego, all that accumulated wealth. Maybe.

One thing is for sure. At 4 a.m. on Christmas morning, 1975, when Sir Charles Chaplin, age eighty-eight, was pronounced "dead of old age" in his twenty-room villa near the eastern tip of Lake Geneva, he had no further use for any of it.

Chaplin's escapades were minor by today's standards of scandalous behavior. As it turned out, they were also innocuous by comparison with the tragic misfortunes of many of his glamorous contemporaries.

Some of the insanity which appeared to grip the brightest stars in the Hollywood firmament was attributed, at least in part, to two things:

the end of World War I and the Volstead Act of 1919 prohibiting the manufacture, distribution, and imbibing of alcoholic beverages.

To the old guard of Hollywood, this was nothing new. Hollywood had been legally dry since 1903! But the movie makers found this curtailment of privilege odious, as did the members of many other professions, not necessarily related to films. The result was widespread bootlegging, of course. Further, hard drugs, not yet illegal, were readily available and both morphine and cocaine were popular remedies for the hangovers induced by over-indulgence in "bathtub gin" or fruity punches laced with 200-proof medicinal alcohol. No wonder that decade made its mark on history as the Roaring Twenties. Not all of the twenties were bad, however . . . not by a long shot. There were some fabulous developments in art, music, literature, industry, and even the movie business.

But for the young film star and the *nouveau riche* movie tycoon, the world was suddenly a gigantic playpen to be filled with toys.

While Chaplin played at being a real-life Don Juan, his fellow Keystone comic, Fatty Arbuckle, an overweight ex-vaudevillean, was trying to recover from the shock of zooming from a $3 per week extra in 1913 to star status at $3 million a year for three films in 1921. He already had everything he wanted, everything money could buy (by his standards). However, before the Labor Day weekend in 1921, he bought a new Pierce Arrow roadster, rented a penthouse suite at the St. Francis Hotel in San Francisco, and invited a full set of "friends" and Hollywood freeloaders to a party there, all expenses paid.

This car was sure sign that Ann Harding, a Broadway thespian, had "gone Hollywood." It was 1930 when Miss Harding was nominated for Holiday.

The sighing mouth. The limp wrist. The hand-dyed marmot furs. For Billie Dove it spelled status. A former Ziegfeld Girl, she was called "The American Beauty" when she starred with Douglas Fairbanks, Sr., in The Black Pirate. A fragile rose, she disappeared in the 1928 wall of sound.

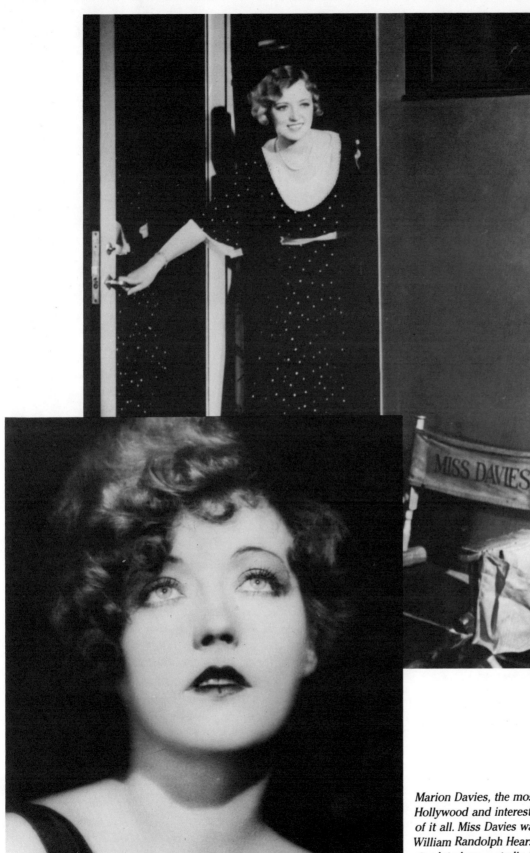

Marion and Norma Shearer as Tyroleans at one
of the scores of costume parties she gave at
San Simeon. Her life came to resemble a
picture post card. But underneath was tragedy
(that she could never marry Hearst) and
shyness (which she would hide with a steadily
growing drinking problem).

This temperature-controlled dressing room was
small stuff compared to the fourteen-room
bungalow Hearst had built for her on the MGM
lot. "If Marion hadn't been talented, all this
would have swamped her," said Hedda Hopper.
Good will could hardly save her from the
withering portrait of her career in Orson
Welles' Citizen Kane.

Marion Davies, the most truly "manufactured star" in
Hollywood and interestingly the city's social queen in spite
of it all. Miss Davies was the paramour of newspaper dictator
William Randolph Hearst, whose press could wither a
star let alone a studio head.

Theda was really the Army's first "pinup"—twenty-five years before Betty Grable. Here she signs incredibly sexy photos of herself naked except for a few long ropes of strategically placed pearls. (Her costume for Serpent of the Nile.) *The smoldering looks on the soldier's faces greeted the vamp wherever she went. The head of a New York department store once told her: "Please don't come in here again, Miss Bara. We'll send the gowns out to you. We can't stand another riot." But Theda switched to sweet roles right after the war, and her fans evaporated. Once a vamp, always a vamp.*

Among the "friends" was Virginia Rappe, a young actress and girl friend of Henry "Pathe" Lehrman, who apparently considered a very drunken Fatty Arbuckle interesting enough to accompany to a bedroom in the suite. There, it was alleged, the two indulged in sexual intercourse, possibly with kinky overtones.

Virginia Rappe was taken ill and died shortly thereafter of what was variously diagnosed as peritonitis, a ruptured bladder, and a chronic disease (possibly venereal) which could have resulted in the same kind of sudden death at any time.

Whatever the diagnosis, Fatty Arbuckle sobered up in jail, charged with murder.

On the first legal go-around, evidence concerning Arbuckle's guilt was so conflicting the Grand Jury refused to indict for murder, opting for manslaughter, despite the emotional objections of the D.A.

When the preliminary hearing was scheduled, some of the most important witnesses claimed to be suffering from amnesia, or had press-

A vamp in sheep's clothing, Theda Bara woos General George Pershing and former President Taft in the very first movie-star day at an Army base in Northern California. The year was 1918—the waning years of the war. Theda's fur hat and white cashmere dress proved to be disappointing to the doughboys, who'd expected to see her as Cleopatra, Carmen, or The Vixen.

ing business elsewhere. Although the D.A. insisted that the unavailability of witnesses was due to bribery or intimidation, he couldn't prove it, so Arbuckle was freed pending trial. Three trials and eight months later, he was acquitted for lack of evidence.

The press exploited every facet of this sensational case. When there was nothing left to say, they resorted to righteous resentment against the enormous earnings of former plumbers and shopgirls who had become movie stars and who were squandering their money in riotous living.

Meantime, not only had Roscoe "Fatty" Arbuckle's multimillion dollar picture contract been cancelled, public outrage was so great and so violent (audiences threw trash at the screen), distributors were obliged to withdraw his films from circulation. The once popular comic was suddenly *persona non grata.* His fair-weather friends faded away; his coterie of freeloaders found greener pastures elsewhere.

The movie business had a peculiar code of ethics. It still does.

Gay young songsters out on a spree—some of Hollywood's biggest heart throbs before their careers started beating. They called it the Alibi Club, a light hearted excuse for drinking and womanizing during the last fling of silent films. Standing (from left) are Director Roland West, Gilbert Roland, Rod La Rocque, and Ben Lyon. Seated, Chester Morris, Buster Collier, and Gary Cooper. As these years faded into the background all of them would veer sharply to the Hollywood right, politically.

Conrad Nagel who could not only "talk" — valuable in itself during the sound panic—he had a voice audiences actually liked.

The foppish Prince David Mdivani, complete with patent leather shoes and a silk ascot, leans down for a peck from his bride, silent superstar Mae Murray. They all said the prince was good in bed, but he used the mattress in a puny attempt to become a Hollywood czar. He spirited Miss Murray away to Europe, spent all her money, and forced her to give up her MGM contract. Then he left for Pola Negri and other greener pastures, leaving Mae without money and without career. (She would die in the motion picture relief home decades later—broke and forgotten).

When you're "in," you're a hero; when you're out, you're a bum. If you're out too long, you might as well be dead. For the next twelve years, Fatty Arbuckle failed at every effort to make a comeback—or a decent living. Finally, in 1932, Warner's offered him a contract to appear in a few short comedies. On April 24, 1933, he celebrated the release of one of them, went to bed—and died in his sleep. He was forty-six years old.

Strangely enough, the Arbuckle tragedy acted like a catalyst on the rest of the industry. It was as though a dam had burst. Vague rumors were suddenly exposed as fact. Some movie stars did get drunk on bootleg booze; some movie stars really were drug addicts; some actors really were drug pushers—and so it went.

As it turned out, 1922 was an extraordinarily significant year in the movie business. That was the year that William Desmond Taylor, handsome actor-director for Famous Players-Lasky, was found shot to death in his own living room on the morning of February 2. To this day, nobody knows for sure why he was killed, or who killed him. Narcotics trafficking may have been involved since Taylor was known to have tried to stop a pusher from supplying a young actress the director was trying to protect. He could have been shot by his girl-friend, Mabel Normand, a protégée of Mack Sennett and an exceedingly popular co-medienne. But, with Mack Sennett at her side, she was completely cleared of any possible complicity. However, shortly after the air had cleared, she and her chauffeur joined a drinking party at the home of Edna Purviance, then Chaplin's leading lady. In the course of the evening, another male guest was shot. It might just as well have been Miss Normand herself. Her movie career was over.

Two other suspects loomed large in the Taylor case, but there were never any convictions. Mary Miles Minter was a young New York actress whom Adolph Zukor had brought to Hollywood as a replacement

for Mary Pickford, who had left Lasky. Pretty little Miss Minter had a mother, an excessively protective mother who frowned on the possible deflowering of her virginal daughter at the hands of director Taylor. Pretty little Miss Minter, on the other hand, seems to have frowned on Mr. Taylor's apparent fondness for Miss Normand. In the long run, nobody won. Taylor remained very, very dead, and both Minter and Normand disappeared permanently from the screen.

Hardly had the public had time to recover from this barrage of scandals when another shocker erupted. Wallace Reid, handsome, talented, athletic, fun-loving, had died in a sanitarium of morphine addiction. He was only thirty years old. The public held Hollywood responsible for this last tragedy. The place itself was a moral disgrace.

Truth to tell, the place was fine—and beautiful. The movie industry was not. Neither were many of its leaders, although a handful of them expressed contrition and promised to clean up their acts in the future.

As it turned out, they had no alternative. Along came Will Hays, a Presbyterian elder then serving as postmaster general in President Harding's cabinet. (Harding, as it turned out, didn't win any special points for moral behavior either!)

Nonetheless, Hays hit the movie industry like a bulldozer. He had full authority to police the morals of the industry and reform its public image . . . and police he did, imposing what was respectfully referred to as a "dictatorship of virtue." Not only were morality clauses

Glass bricks and frosted windows helped make "The 'IT' Cafe" the in place to go in the late twenties. But the real draw was Jazz Baby Clara Bow, the "it girl" who stopped in a couple of times a week and mingled with the guests. Clara finally closed the cafe during the Depression, but she was much richer from dishing up burgers. It was one of Hollywood's weirder investments but there were others: Billie Burke financed a salad dressing; Mary Pickford built and ran a miniature golf course; De Mille had a 1,700 acre pheasant ranch; Alan Ladd opened a hardware store; and George Murphy, before he had political aspirations, packaged and sold "Murphy's Rubbing Linament" using a compound invented by his dad.

(Above)
A rare view of Sunset Boulevard at Crescent Heights Boulevard in 1935, this semi-aerial shot shows the whole hotel/bungalow complex of the Garden of Allah, where a small bar was reserved for such serious drinkers as Bob Benchley, Charles Butterworth, F. Scott Fitzgerald, et al. In the piano bar, however, Jesse Stacey played jazz and swing on piano. Occasionally, an aspiring young actor named Jack Lemmon sat in for him, and according to Stacey, "was damned good."

(Left)
In 1940, the Garden Of Allah Hotel boasted a guest register which had included almost every major film star in the Hollywood firmament as a permanent or transient resident sometime between 1918, when the 3½-acre estate was The Garden of Alla, the spacious home of actress Alla Nazimova, and 1959, when the complex was razed.

7540

The Beverly Hills Hotel, already a pink palace, opened in 1912 far from the center of Hollywood. But it lured the manager of the Hollywood Hotel, Mrs. Margaret Anderson—along with her chef, her recipes, and, most important, her famous clientele—Swanson, Pickford, et al. Built by the Rodeo Land and Cattle Company, the hotel had caged monkeys, screeching parrots, and an absolutely irresistible setting. It's still pink, still famous, and still full of stars—a durable throwback to Hollywood's golden era.

inserted in player contracts, extras in search of picture work had to join the Central Casting Agency. As members, they were no longer obliged to submit to the casting couch as a prerequisite for work. On the other hand, unless a prostitute could prove registration with Central Casting, there was no hope of having a vagrancy charge dismissed on the grounds that the girl in question was hanging around outside the studio gates simply as an extra in search of work as a movie walk-on.

Perhaps to purify the screen and set itself up as a force for moral good, the Hays office turned away from the sex and sadism of the twenties to give its full support to Cecil B. De Mille's classic opus *The Ten Commandments.* Nobody seems to have questioned the dubious morality of actress Estelle Taylor's interpretation of the Biblical Miriam's adoration of the Golden Calf. Miss Taylor later married Jack Dempsey—heavyweight boxing champ. They did not live happily ever after, either.

IV PROHIBITION AND THE GREAT DEPRESSION:
Hollywood Style

Lake Hollywood as it looked in 1930—with mansions climbing the slopes that were carefully being destroyed by bulldozers under the direction of dam builder William Mulholland.

(Left)
Alla Nazimova, a silent screen star who made her fortune playing exotic darkhaired vamps, donned a blonde wig in 1926 and produced her own version of Salome with Warren Williams as co-star.

I t should be obvious that since some sort of balance is an essential component of survival, not all of the nuts who slipped into Hollywood were directly associated with the film industry. Indirectly associated, perhaps, especially after November 11, 1918, when the Armistice was signed. On that day, in one decisive move, an international covey of political powers gathered together and in a solemn scratching of pens not only put an end to the hostilities of World War I, "the war to end all wars," but actually believed that in so doing they had also "made the world safe for democracy," whatever that meant.

In Hollywood, it was business as usual. Democracy was dandy and a good thing for politicians to talk about, but democracies couldn't make moving pictures. Producers made them. And producers had to be dictators, for obvious reasons. Therefore, dictators made films. They still do.

Meanwhile, in the first flush of postwar euphoria, the "democratic principle" was translated to mean "the greatest good for the greatest number." Out of that came Prohibition, a clearly-defined constitutional amendment which in essence prohibited the manufacture, sale, transport, and consumption of all alcoholic beverages except for medicinal purposes.

The impact of this legislation on the *nouveau riche* of Hollywood was only momentarily traumatic. The old guard simply shrugged. Hollywood had been legally dry since 1903 when one of its first city ordinances instituted prohibition and banned the sale of booze in the then newly-built Hollywood Hotel, along with Blondeau's Tavern and other friendly neighborhood bistros.

But for the rest of the community, after the first shock of having to cope with legally-induced short supply, the changes in lifestyle were no more influenced by this new law than the "Jesus Freaks" of later postwar movements were to correct the moral decadence of those eras—with one major difference.

Prohibition did breed bootleggers. Bootleggers, in turn, contributed mightily to the creation of the legendary Roaring Twenties, although some of that roaring was anguished. Together with dope pushers, gamblers, rum runners, pimps, and hit men, they found cordial welcome in Hollywood. Further, the coastal waters of the Pacific provided easy points of entry for all kinds of illicit products and services.

On the sea, beyond the three-mile limit west of almost any coastal point from San Diego to Santa Barbara, floating crap games (and almost any other contraband pleasure one might wish) were quite literally afloat on specially outfitted ships. Launches picked up and delivered their live cargo from the far end of darkened fishing piers, or scooped them off pleasure yachts anchored at a comfortable distance west of the shoreline, always with one eye cocked for Coast Guard cutters which might possibly bear down on them if payoffs were late—or inadequate. If, as did happen from time to time, the situation threatened to overheat, there was always the Mexican border, only a stone's throw away.

Not everything was afloat, however. Not by a long shot. Hoods on the lam from the law in major eastern and midwestern cities found easy refuge on an isolated sprawl of acreage adjacent to Hollywood, but west of it. The land, as such, owed allegiance to nobody, it seemed.

It wasn't a city and didn't belong to any one individual. It was simply known as the Los Angeles County Strip, which meant it had no genuine ruling body, other than the county board of supervisors, whose attentions were occupied elsewhere.

There were no police departments to contend with, only a handful of deputy sheriffs who had other more important areas to focus on. It was pretty and hilly and had its own unpaved two-lane main artery called Sunset Boulevard, winding west at the foot of the Hollywood Hills, providing easy access to the valley and the now-developing canyons— the same canyons Tiburcio Vasquez, Hollywood's first romantic bandit, had used for escape from the law.

In the early twenties, nobody suspected the role this strip of Sunset was to play in the creation of the glamour that was supposed to be Hollywood's own. However, like Hollywood itself, the world-famous

For Christmas of 1938, Hollywood perpetuated the industry's preoccupation with stars and canopied the boulevard with hundreds of the lighted symbols. Pantages Theater, another popular "première palace," was showing "2 Great Features"—Smashing the Spy Ring, *starring Ralph Bellamy and Fay Wray, along with* Little Tough Guys in Society *with Mischa Auer, Mary Boland, and a supporting actor named Edward Everett Horton. In 1943 the Academy of Motion Picture Arts moved its oh-so-exclusive award ceremonies from hotel banquet rooms to the Pantages Theater, where for the first time in history, they were open to the public.*

Warner Brothers Pictures in 1926, looking peaceful and a bit sleepy-headed. But behind those colonial walls, engineers were already at work recording the musical score for the first talkie, The Jazz Singer. *The three Warner brothers had already let their secret slip out by providing John Barrymore's* Don Juan *with a symphonic background. But nobody paid the slightest attention until Al Jolson said (from the screen)—"You ain't heard nothin' yet."*

Vanished glory. These metal and glass Christmas trees and 800 stars helped Hollywood Boulevard live up to its title as Christmas capital of America. They called the boulevard Santa Claus Lane in those years, and movie stars like Claudette Colbert and Errol Flynn rode in a holiday parade. In the seventies, Hollywood—a shadow of its former self—initiated an effort to recapture the parade's big star quality and excitement. But by then television stars outnumbered movie stars.

Grauman's Chinese Theatre, destined to become the most glamorous of all movie palaces in Hollywood and out of it, set its own history in motion in May 1927 with the invitational première of Cecil B. De Mille's King of Kings. Now famous the world over for its collection of movie-star footprints, handprints, and signatures impressed into the concrete blocks of its patio, the first such prints were actually those of Grauman himself who, while inspecting the nearly completed building, accidentally stepped on the wet cement, or so the story goes.

Sunset Strip is still nowhere to be found on street sign, map, or document. Officially it doesn't exist, although it occupies 1.9 square miles of unincorporated county territory, bisected by twelve blocks of Sunset Boulevard and bounded on the west by Beverly Hills.

Except for ranchers and ranch hands, an occasional wagon trundling along with merchandise for delivery somewhere, there were few signs of life along the Sunset Strip until 1924 when, for no apparent reason, a few commercial buildings made their appearance.

In the boom years preceding the stock market crash and the Great Depression, the Strip attracted generous investment in posh apartment hotels like the Chateau Marmont and residential highrises like the Sunset Towers. Nightclubs and private clubs nestled together at the foot of the hills of West Hollywood like so many better mousetraps created to attract the rich and famous. Both in turn proved irresistibly attractive to such humorless members of America's criminal subculture as Frank Costello, Jack Dragna, Bugsy Siegel, and Mickey Cohen, a typical admixture of underworld luminaries who invested in the Sunset Strip one way or the other.

Meanwhile, there were some very sane things going on in Hollywood—and east of it. In 1915, Vitagraph Pictures had bought an eleven-acre tract at Prospect Avenue (Hollywood Boulevard) and Talmadge Street, out of the Hollywood mainstream and away from the high winds which were interfering with picture-making in their Santa Monica studio. Five years later, the company had invested an additional $200,000 into the lot in order to provide dressing rooms and other modern conveniences for the stars, including individual shower baths.

The first five years of the 1920s in Hollywood were loaded with this kind of pretentiousness, not a lot of which made sense. On March 28, 1920, glamorous movie star Douglas Fairbanks, having been divorced by his first wife, Anna Beth Sully, mother of Doug Fairbanks, Jr., married rich and glamorous movie star Mary Pickford, who had divorced actor Owen Moore. Whereupon, they lived happily for several years in Pickfair, their legendary mansion where they set up the social ladder and ruled from the throne room at the top.

That same year, four brothers named Warner arrived in Hollywood as filmmakers after abandoning their Chicago scrapmetal and wholesale butcher business. At first interested only in exhibition, the brothers entered production with a film dealing with venereal disease, starring Jack L. Warner, the youngest brother. The movie could scarcely have been called a smash hit, even though it did have a competent supporting player in Ben Lyon. In 1925 Jack Warner gave up his acting career and the Warner Brothers opted for a big gamble . . . they bought Vitagraph's eleven acres.

In 1921, just to keep the events of the half-decade straight, Fatty Arbuckle blew his career with a drunken orgy in San Francisco, and Rudolph Valentino debuted in *The Four Horsemen of the Apocalypse*.

In 1922, Famous Players-Lasky director William Desmond Taylor, fully dressed, expired on the floor of his Hollywood cottage due to an errant bullet. Movie star Mabel Normand, one of Charlie Chaplin's leading

Gale Sondergaard wore a black monkey-fur coat and a flaming red dress to this première of Zola, called the dressiest première in Hollywood history. Warner's ordered all their stars and character actors to attend the opening at the Carthay Circle near Wilshire Boulevard. The ordinary première in Hollywood cost from $5,500 to $10,000, but real extravaganzas such as this one cost as much as $50,000, with two-thirds of that money being spent on lights. It cost $3,000 for fresh flowers alone for Zola.

Grauman's Egyptian Theatre, Hollywood's first genuine "picture palace" was outrageously theatrical from the beginning. Bristling with "authentic" hieroglyphs, sphinx-heads, and other artifacts, short-skirted Egyptian "guards" patrolled the wide walls above the patio where, from time to time, live monkeys cavorted in cages for the amusement of passersby.

(Below)
Famous bubble dancer, Sally Rand, appeared without her bubble and with clothes in Hollywood's Santa Claus Lane Parade. Miss Rand, here with the then fashionable "Marion Davies" pageboy, gained fame when she danced nude behind a bubble for a Prohibition party in Chicago.

ladies, among others, was allegedly involved. Despite investigations, evidence continued to disappear and the case was never resolved.

However, while Desmond Taylor and Fatty Arbuckle were scandals to drool over, the public was more horrified than titillated by the sudden death of handsome, romantic, athletic Wally Reid, who died in 1923 of morphine addiction. Into the breach rode the Hays Office, the Sir Lancelots of law, order, and morality in films. That did it.

Although scandalous sudden death in the film business continued at a fairly orderly rate, nobody appeared to be indispensable, although a few moguls were missed more than others. Thomas Harper Ince, age forty-three, for example, was missed. He was one of the cinema's greatest artists, on a par with Griffith for sheer creativity. He died suddenly after dining with newspaper tycoon William Randolph Hearst aboard his yacht. It was thought that he was happily planning to direct Marion Davies, Hearst's mistress, in some stories adapted from *Cosmopolitan* magazine, although there is no strong evidence to indicate that Hearst heartily approved of the project. Somehow, in the champagne celebration which followed the discussion, Thomas Ince expired, ostensibly of thrombosis. There were other explanations, too, of course. He had ulcers, for example. But what he did not have was a long life.

Meanwhile, in the real world down on the mainland, another newspaper publisher named Harry Chandler was involving himself in

This baby-sized colonial office accurately portrays the size and importance of Metro Pictures, founded in 1914 as an independent filmmaker. The West Coast offices were deliberately small because the Metro execs in the East were not sold on either California or Hollywood. The small studio sent Francis X. Bushman to Hollywood in 1914 to make one picture a month. But his letters home complained constantly of fog. Besides, opined Bushman, "This is semitropical country and Hollywoodsmen aren't used to working that much. The minute we turned our backs they were out in the sun or playing billiards. It'll never go."

Bette Davis and Errol Flynn pretended to be civil to each other long enough to get through the première of Elizabeth and Essex. But Davis often complained that the premières were a bigger production than the movies themselves. Wilson Mizner referred to the Hollywood openings as "bloody Indian raids in top hat and tails."

In July 1942, although wartime blackout regulations had doused klieg-lighted premières for the duration, Warner Brothers retained the tradition of glamorous openings by introducing Yankee Doodle Dandy to the public with a "$5,000,000 Band Première." James Cagney won the Academy's best actor award for his performance, and picked up a wartime version of the Oscar—a gold-painted plaster replica. This was the year Greer Garson's acceptance speech for her role in Mrs. Miniver ran a full hour, the longest such speech in Academy history.

Max Factor, movie makeup pioneer in 1928 enacted a dual role as makeup artist (on actress Gladys McConnell) and promoter of the safe and luxurious travel afforded by Maddux Airlines, one of the first companies to offer scheduled flights along with special charter service. Factor who had started in the wig business, progressed from one-man makeup artist to cosmetic-manufacturing tycoon whose mammoth company sold out to Norton Simon for millions in the mid-1970s.

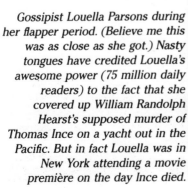

Gossipist Louella Parsons during her flapper period. (Believe me this was as close as she got.) Nasty tongues have credited Louella's awesome power (75 million daily readers) to the fact that she covered up William Randolph Hearst's supposed murder of Thomas Ince on a yacht out in the Pacific. But in fact Louella was in New York attending a movie première on the day Ince died.

another form of good works. In the company of two fellow investors, M.H. Sherman and S.H. Woodruff, he set some steam shovels in motion in the peaceful hills of Beachwood Canyon, leveling and filling and creating pads for the construction of a whole new tract of luxurious homes adjoining the wilderness acreage of Griffith Park. On Mount Lee, the hill above the tract and west of it, the gentlemen ecologists decided to erect a sign which would be visible for miles, as far south as Wilshire Boulevard in those smog-free days.

The responsibility for the sign landed on the shoulders of a young commercial artist named John D. Roche, who lettered the name of the tract—HOLLYWOODLAND—on a combination drawing and photographic blowup of the mountain.

Chandler bought the project which involved construction of thirteen letters, fifty feet high and thirty feet wide, formulated of telegraph poles hauled up the rugged hill by mules, aided and abetted by

About 1927, Lloyd Wright became involved in creating the first shell for the Hollywood Bowl, when it became apparent that the bowl might be put to a more continuing theatrical use. This bowl, sporting a Southwest Indian motif, owed its wooden materials to another show, Robin Hood, whose set was dismantled and adapted for this need. According to Wright, the whole thing represented an investment of about $8,500. And a great deal of time.

Hollywood Bowl's second shell, also designed by Lloyd Wright, son of the famous architect Frank Lloyd Wright, was put to use in the summer of 1928. Easy to dismantle and acoustically correct, Wright's concept was nonetheless "improved upon" in subsequent versions, infuriating Wright to the point of threatening to sue.

McKinley Mortuary, on Sunset Boulevard just at the foot of Horn Avenue, was noted for a couple of things. For one, it was ornamented by a clock which had no hands. It was continually threatened by brakeless cars sailing driverless down the hill. Most importantly, this was the mortuary from which John Barrymore's body was stolen and delivered to a swivel chair in Errol Flynn's home by a couple of his buddies who waited drunkenly to witness Flynn's reaction upon his return hours later. (Flynn, at that point in time, had a strong heart!)

Schwab's Pharmacy, even in 1947, when this photo was taken, wasn't much to look at, but there wasn't an actor or actress, writer, director, producer, or gaffer in Hollywood who didn't know that the coffee was fresh and hot and, if you were down on your luck, you could probably eat and drink now—and pay later. Maybe.

between fifty and a hundred Mexican laborers who dug deep holes with pickaxes and shovels . . . total cost, $21,000. When the sign was completed, 4,000 light bulbs made it visible for miles at night. Unfortunately, the bright commercial aspects of the sign aggravated later audiences to the Hollywood Bowl, who found the blinking lights unpleasantly distracting. In due course, lights were vandalized—some stolen, some shot out by sportsmen who found them irresistible targets for beebee guns. Maintenance was erratic at best, and by 1939 all efforts to hold it together had been abandoned . . . the "H" fell down. Somebody put it back up. Then the whole "LAND" portion of the sign slid downhill, never to be replaced. The white paint peeled—and word was out that the sign simply reflected the fading glories of Hollywood, one-time movie capital of the world.

However, jumping ahead a few decades, by the end of 1979, a whole new HOLLYWOOD sign had been built, of durable steel and by public subscription. Large sums were contributed by magazine publishers, recording companies, recording artists, Gene Autry's TV station, etc. Missing completely . . . motion pictures . . . not one single major film company, actor, or producer contributed a dime to that romantic HOLLYWOOD sign on Mount Lee. Total cost, $249,300.

So a pile of tin and wood was transformed into an international shrine. This was just another salute to the triumph of trivia—an art form that gave publicists the power to turn the size of a star's waist or her shade of lipstick into an American news event.

And as the bulldozers moved in to level Hollywood's most precious resource—the hills—the movie moguls found that they had the power to make or break superstars. No longer did they wait for the public to make a star; they took a youngster right off the train; gave her a new name, a different hair color, a made-to-order life story and then shoved her into as many pictures as possible before the newness wore off. When men like Louis B. Mayer decided that actors and actresses owed everything to them personally, it was in the cards that Hollywood would become a despotic kingdom ruled by men determined that their creative vision would dominate the making of what they considered to be their movies. The barons of Hollywood had worked themselves up from the street. Most of them were impoverished Russian Jewish immigrants who had spent their youths scrambling for a living any way they could. Mayer had been a roving junk dealer; Paramount's Jesse Lasky panned for gold in Alaska; Sam Goldwyn (true name, Goldfish) started as a glove cutter; Darryl Zanuck loaded bananas on the New York docks; Jack L. Warner worked as a cobbler. The business acumen they acquired to survive gave them an edge over the competition when they moved into vaudeville and then into the new medium of film.

Inevitably, their hard-driving autocratic personalities were transferred to the studios they built. Individual actors were seen as raw material to be polished into gleaming parts of an overall product created by and belonging to the men in charge. Sometimes they would fashion their human raw material into masterpieces, like Greta Garbo. Other times the emerging shape would not meet their expectations and would

The famous Frank Lloyd Wright house in Barnsdall Park. Oil heiress Aline Barnsdall brought the architectural genius out to Hollywood in 1923 and gave him free rein. The result, patterned after the Mesa silhouette of the Pueblo Indians, was called Hollyhock House after Aline's favorite flower. Unlike another early example of great local architecture, Irving Gill's Dodge House, this estate was saved from the wrecker's ball. It is now owned by the city of Los Angeles, which uses it, appropriately, for cultural purposes.

A masterpiece of Hollywood architecture crafted by John Delario, Castillo del Lago still sits on the Hollywood hillside above Lake Hollywood.

be callously discarded, a sacrifice to the quest for a superior overall product. The studios, often ruthless, always reflected the vision of their creators.

During those early decades, however, the operation of these human erector sets had a degree of charm.

Stars of the silver screen were literally discovered walking down the street. For instance, Samuel Goldwyn got his first glimpse of Vilma Banky in a jammed Budapest train station—he was on his way back to the states, and she was on her way to the opera.

She had black and silver ostrich feathers soaring out of her hat and about 10,000 black jet beads glittering on her Paris gown. "She was the most breathtaking woman I'd ever seen," said Goldwyn. "But she didn't speak English and I didn't speak any of those other languages." That proved to be no stumbling block for Goldwyn, who found an attorney who spoke both languages and signed her to a long-term contract right there on the grand staircase in the train station.

Vilma Banky took her time coming to America (completing six movies in her own country first). When she did get to Hollywood, Goldwyn was in New York, so the Hungarian star just collected her paycheck and dined out each evening. And did she ever dine well! "I took one look at her and started to ask if she was the right Vilma Banky," said Goldwyn. "She had blown up like a balloon, and I despaired of ever getting her back down to movie star weight." Miss Banky was only learning about two words a day, so it took Goldwyn some time to find out what was wrong. It turned out that Vilma was simply unable to

Barnsdall Park in 1925—shortly after an entire forest of olive trees were planted around the Hollyhock House. The estate—which has come down intact—is virtually the only large oasis of greenery in central Hollywood.

By the early 40s, this building on Sunset Boulevard had been remodeled to accommodate Cafe La Rue, whose tasteful elegance, fine food, and high prices attracted the most affluent film folk and socialites, as well as a fair number of freeloading press who paid off press agents, stars and the restaurant with column items beginning, "Seen dining at La Rue . . . (Ciro's, Mocambo, Trocadero, etc.)

Lillian Millicent "Peg" Entwhistle, a successful graduate of the New York Theatre Guild about 1930, answered Hollywood's call for stage actors as "talkies" gained popularity. Still, parts were scarce. Almost broke, in 1932 she moved into the Hollywood Studio Club where telephone service was included with the rent. Then, thoroughly discouraged, on a warm September evening she headed for the Hollywood Hills and the peak of Mount Lee. From the top of the "H" in the "Hollywoodland" sign, then the highest pinnacle of Hollywood, she leaped toward the lights of the city. Her body was found in the morning on the rugged side of the mountain more than fifty feet below that mocking sign.

(Opposite)
Patrik Longan, a geologist who became rich off the oil boom in the South Bay, built this white castle overlooking Lake Hollywood as a dream house for his wife. He spent a hundred thousand just to grade the site and put in an elevated ramp to reach the hilltop. The Longans named it Castillo del Lago and had just finished furnishing the palace when Mrs. Longan died suddenly. Longan abandoned the house, sold it, and moved down to the Wilshire area. The house shows up again as a gambling den and speakeasy run by Bugsy Siegel. In 1979 it was restored by the Donald Wilfongs so thoroughly that the couple spent two years finding and buying back fixtures and furniture from the original house.

decipher the California menus; she just pointed and packed on about five pounds a week.

Goldwyn carefully coached her—teaching her to order only the low calorie dishes. Vilma Banky was later to say that she ate little more than pineapple wedges and lamb chops for almost six months. But it worked, and Banky went on to become a superstar. (Retiring, however, with the coming of sound, she married silent screen lover Rod LaRocque, and had a happy marriage that lasted half a century.)

Sometimes the Goldwyn formula (which created Lucille Ball and Susan Hayward) would backfire. The producer spent a million dollars of his own money to make a star out of another European, Anna Sten. He put her into one expensive vehicle after another—only giving in after the fourth flop. "Who knows? Maybe it was the wrong year for Hungarians," Goldwyn would say.

The movie power brokers often used as much ingenuity and creativity to tear down the stars they had so carefully created.

Mayer proved again and again that he was a one man wrecking crew. "When he destroyed them, they never got up again," said Joan Crawford. Two of his most tragic casualties made history by their sorrowful crashes from the heights to the depths. And those two, Mae Murray and Francis X. Bushman did everything right—acted well, kept their looks, and played the fan magazine game. But they committed the unpardonable sin; they unwittingly slighted L.B. (Bushman by answering a phone in Italy with a curt, profane sentence, not knowing it was Mayer. And Murray by walking out of her MGM contract to take a honeymoon.)

Bushman, the most popular matinee idol in the twenties, had become a millionaire and was living a picture-book life with his wife Beverly Bayne, who had played Juliet to his Romeo in 1916. When MGM signed him to play Messala to Ramon Novarro's Ben Hur, the performance was called one of the five best of the silent era. Then Bushman picked up the phone in Rome and blurted out the insult, thinking it was his valet.

Mayer, in Italy to try and salvage the runaway budget of *Ben Hur,* vowed that day he would hound Bushman out of the business. It was a promise he kept—aided greatly by the coming of sound and the stock market crash. (What is surprising is that Mayer dropped Bushman when the star was at the zenith of his popularity. "My husband was just a product to him, nothing more," Beverly Bayne was to say a half century later.)

Mae Murray's fall assumed Greek tragedy proportions. She had dropped completely out of sight (not even included in "What Ever Became Of") when she was found wandering through the winter streets of St. Louis in 1964. It took city police twenty-four hours to confirm her identity. Even then, nobody came forward to pay her hotel bill until the Salvation Army guaranteed the $13.50 for the night and then put her on the plane to Los Angeles (where she lived another year in the Motion Picture Country Home).

Called the "first international glamour girl" in 1925, Miss Murray

With a private manicurist doing his nails and a character actor at his ear, Cecil B. De Mille, a true Hollywood dictator directs filming of Northwest Mounted Police, 1940. "He wore puttees and thumped around doing some very extravagant things," says author Adela Rogers St. Johns. "And his office was like a cathedral with stained glass windows just above his head. How did he see himself? Well, I think he gave God first place, but right under there was Mr. De Mille."

C.B. rarely indulged in moments as silly as this one—when he was made an honorary Iroquois Indian. Mostly, at Paramount (which he helped found), De Mille treated big stars like so many rickshaw drivers. Henry Hathaway, later to become a major director himself, started his career by carrying C.B.'s chair around the set. "When he sat down, the chair better be there—Mr. De Mille didn't look . . . just sat." One day, when the crew was filming near the ocean, De Mille walked out into the surf to check for an angle. All six toadies, including Hathaway with his chair, waded out until they were waist deep. "He might put out his hand . . . so we felt we better be there," said Hathaway.

(Opposite, bottom)
Through this enormous gate passed "more stars than there are in the heavens," the contract players of Metro-Goldwyn-Mayer. The ever-ready limousine waited at the constant beck and call of Louis B. Mayer, and the catwalk led to the dressing rooms of Greta Garbo, Jean Harlow, Joan Crawford, Norma Shearer, and Jeanette MacDonald. People who look forlornly back to those salad days have forgotten the scent of fear that always loomed above the studio which even cut Crawford and Garbo adrift during tough times.

Somewhere in the middle of this mad house are Judy Garland and Mickey Rooney performing "Way Out West, on Western Avenue" for the MGM cameras. The film was Gershwin's Girl Crazy, 1942. The musical was set at a dude ranch so MGM didn't bother going on location; they just built the dude ranch right there on sound stage seven. Busby Berkeley is the director behind the camera; he was a genius but a creative perfectionist, hounding Garland with retakes. About this time she started her trip down the highway of pills. Contrary to rumor, MGM did not give her pills as part of her job. They just saw to it that the studio medics made them available if anyone needed them. Judy, like many others, found uppers inviting at the end of an eighteen-hour day.

was making more than $3 million a year. She came to the MGM lot in a gold and silver plated Rolls Royce—fitted with a wet bar and completely carpeted inside with sable and ermine. After her most famous film, *The Merry Widow,* was released, she became known as "the girl with the bee-stung lips."

She walked off the lot to get married at the height of her popularity. Mayer sent her a cable to come back immediately. She answered: "Have a heart, it's my honeymoon." "She'll never work for me—or for any other major studio—ever again," Mayer told her agent. Again, he kept his word.

But with the thirties a new, tougher brand of stars moved to the top ranks at the studios. Bette Davis, Joan Crawford, Clark Gable, Carole Lombard, Joan Blondell—these newcomers had walked in over the graves of the old elite. And they learned from the past mistakes.

Davis fought her way out of a tyrannical studio standoff (in which Jack L. Warner forced her into "B" movies) by fleeing to England and refusing to return until she had script approval. Once back, Warner

Jazz Baby Clara Bow hugs the latest and swankiest radio set for an advertisement of the twenties. Ironically, radio was to seal Clara's doom as it forced the movies into sound—a revolution her career was too fragile to survive. The actress would probably be able to appreciate the renaissance now being given to her films. She died in 1965 in a private sanitarium less than a mile from the studio her movies helped build—Paramount.

would do anything to keep from confronting her face to face. Miss Davis made him so paranoid that he stationed one of his secretaries in front of a window. When the secretary could see Davis heading up the street— usually with her fists clenched—she pushed a button and Warner could flee out the back door.

Over at MGM, Mayer was getting some of his medicine thrown back at him by Garbo and Crawford. In one particularly stormy confrontation, Garbo would not sign her new contract until she had script approval, co-star approval, and approval of her directors. Mayer tried to give her a compromise contract with only about forty percent of what she had asked for. "What do you think of this?" he said, handing over the contract with tricks written in—far down in the fine print. Garbo took the document over to the window and began reading it paragraph by paragraph. Two hours later Mayer again asked, "Well, what do you think?" Garbo tossed the compromise contract onto the desk, saying: "I think I go home now—home to Sweden." Needless to say, Garbo got her way.

Mary at thirty-six, a fading flapper with over-painted lips and false spit curls. Hollywood has always ruthlessly exploited rather than protected its greatest stars. She had been Pollyanna for two decades. Now, obviously on the advice of some United Artists executive (worried over the dwindling Pickford ticket sales) "America's Sweetheart" suffered public indignities. She would never try for a third comeback. She hid away: "I never want my fans to see me grow old."

(Above)
Wally Reid and his son Billy
poolside in what appears to
have been happier days.

Paramount commissioned this 1920 Christmas morning photo of
Wally Reid, his wife Dorothy Davenport, and their son Billy. The
studio was aware, that early, that Reid was hopelessly hooked.
Director Henry Hathaway remembers Wally's last day on the set:
"He sort of fumbled about and bumped into a chair. Then he sat
down on the floor and started to cry. They propped him up in the
chair (to continue filming) but he just tipped over. Finally, finally
they called the ambulance."

Wally Reid, the Robert Redford
of his day; the first golden boy
of the movies; a star of such
personal magnetism that a New
York debutante once traded an
emerald necklace for a look at
his dressing room. From 1910
(when he made The Phoenix at
age 19) until an ambulance
carried him from the set of
Thirty Days in 1922, Reid made
more pictures and more money
for Paramount than any star
before or since.

This still from a doomed Arbuckle film, started when he was charged, was believed destroyed. But Paramount researchers found it in 1979. Earlier, the studio had destroyed all remaining Arbuckle negatives without waiting for the final court decision: He was acquitted. And not only acquitted, but with this apology: "Acquittal is not enough for Roscoe Arbuckle. There was not the slightest proof to connect him in any way with the commission of a crime. A great injustice was done him."

Constance Talmadge, who made ten million dollars making silent comedies, gave up without a fight when talkies were born. Her sister, the more famous Norma Talmadge, suffered through very early talkies—dreadfully exposing the heavy Brooklyn accent she had in common with Norma.

(Far left)
Strange structure in the 8400 block of Lookout Mountain Avenue is reputed to have been the home of Fatty Arbuckle, comedy star of silent films in the twenties. Caught up in a sensational scandal involving the sordid death of a young actress, Arbuckle was never convicted of complicity, but his career—and his life—were destroyed. This house remains, as uncertainly his as the degree of his involvement in one of Hollywood's juiciest scandals to date.

(Left)
Mabel Normand, here looking at Picture Show with her portrait on the cover, had been seen slipping out the door of William Desmond Taylor's bungalow the night he was killed. A few months later her chauffeur was found standing over the body of Cortland S. Dines, a Hollywood millionaire. Mabel's pistol was in his hand.

Mary Miles Minter, here being menaced by a lecherous screen lawyer, was the silent films' second golden girl, after Mary Pickford. She was pushed to great prominence over the broken psyche of Fatty Arbuckle when Paramount rushed to fill the gap left by the silent comedian. She seemed a safe bet until her passionate love letters were found in William Desmond Taylor's private cassock. Many people feel that Minter's mother killed Taylor. But evidence indicates that it was really a sordid killing involving sex and drugs.

William Desmond Taylor as he determined posterity would know him. He said he was a Britisher, a former Royal Army officer, but after he was murdered in 1922 Hollywood learned he was really William Deane Tanner, a humble Irishman.

Joan Crawford was equally strident. When publicist Henry Rogers (who founded Rogers and Cowan), was asked to take over Crawford's PR, he found her already equipped with advanced public relations skills.

The actress had just left MGM for good when she summoned Rogers to her Brentwood mansion. The publicist knocked on the door and faced an English butler who told him: "Take your shoes off—Miss Crawford does not allow shoes in here." With a wave of his proper hand the butler showed Rogers through a kitchen carpeted in white, up a white hall, and into a white bedroom.

Joan was sitting in a dressing room paneled entirely with Viennese mirrors. She was reading a script while one woman gave her a manicure and another crouched on the floor giving her a pedicure. A young male hairdresser hovered somewhere behind and above her.

She looked Rogers over, handed him a typed agenda in three copies and started talking. "Call me Joan," she said, "I'll call you Henry. You're planning to give me ideas. Well, I don't need them. I'm a better press agent for Joan Crawford than anyone else could ever be. Let me do the thinking. You do the doing. I'm getting ready for dinner now, so I won't have time to talk to you any longer. Please get started and follow through on what I have indicated."

Rogers found out that Crawford even scheduled her times in the bathroom and her most personal of needs. Looking over one of the famous Crawford schedules, Rogers asked, "What does 'time for Philip' mean?" (Philip Terry was her husband at the time.) Joan smiled and turned toward her publicist. "Well, we're good friends, Henry, so I'll tell

At 2450 Canyon Boulevard, this rocky entrance tantalizes the imagination, for it was in this immediate area that Houdini, the Great Escape Artist, once lived. Next door, so the story goes, the Green Virgin moved in her mysterious ways. Both houses were destroyed by fire, leaving only entrance stairs to document their onetime existence. Then, whose stairs are these?

Mary Miles Minter and her attorney shown here during Mary's attempt to regain the fortune her mother spent.

Douglas Fairbanks had his costumes cut tighter, his hair tinted darker, and his co-stars portrayed younger. (For example Mary Astor at seventeen in Don Q., Son of Zorro.*) Doug had headed over the fatal chasm for a swashbuckler; he'd turned forty and had the tired face to show it. The Pickford-Fairbanks marriage collapsed along with their careers, after the disastrous* Taming of the Shrew.

Doug and Mary; in the twenties everybody supposed they would drift together happily ever after. That was to be the movies' first cruel joke. Doug's midriff began to go flabby, and no amount of exercise would turn back the clock. And Mary? The first gray hairs appeared bringing a leaden silence to Sundays at Pickfair. Doug Sr. and Doug Jr. followed the sun, Mary went up for a nap, and Junior's bride Joan Crawford remembered sitting in the still living room lost in silence for four hours.

you. Time for Philip is the time we make love."

The publicist left the meeting shaking his head: "Being well organized was admirable. But scheduling on paper in advance time for lovemaking with one's own husband was too much for me."

Two years after Crawford met with Rogers, her public relations campaign was paying off. She was back bigger than ever with her own personal style. Not only did she win an Oscar (for *Mildred Pierce*), but she had gone from "box office poison" to number eight at the box office.

And her tactics were to form part of a legend for new stars—enabling actresses like Marilyn Monroe and Jayne Mansfield to top their studios at their own game.

Meanwhile, the dictators reigned. They would bow to an occasional Crawford or Davis, if it enabled them to make the movies they wanted, but usually their rule was all-powerful.

Real stagecoaches rolled down Hollywood Boulevard to Grauman's Chinese Theatre in 1939 for the opening of Stagecoach with John Wayne as the Ringo Kid. From a thirty-two-year-old also-ran, the movie catapulted Wayne to superstardom.

John Wayne, who made his film debut in The Big Trail in 1931, and Constance Cummings, who co-starred with George Raft in 1932 in Night After Night.

V HOLLYWOOD'S HEYDAY: The Glamorous Thirties

Mary Pickford's hands were trembling. She inched up to the microphone that had been set up in the center of her lavish dressing room on the United Artists lot.

Before she opened her mouth to speak she looked over to Douglas Fairbanks for comfort. He smiled reassuringly, his hands clenched at his sides.

Finally she began to talk—almost in a whisper.

With each word that she spoke, the voice of America's Sweetheart got stronger.

At the end of ten minutes Mary was talking confidently into the mike—and therefore to a radio audience across America—as if radio were an old friend (which it would prove not to be).

115

Judy and Mickey with dear old father figure Louis B. Mayer helping Judy cut her sixteenth birthday cake. It's a safe bet, however, that Daddy Lou snatched the cake away as soon as the press photographers were out of sight . . . he had long ago put Garland on a forced diet to peel ten pounds off. Chefs in the commissary were ordered to give her nothing but chicken broth which, good though it was, kept Judy's appetite frazzled.

The front gates of MGM at the beginning of World War II; a lot of the old glamour was gone—along with dismissed stars Crawford, Garbo, and Shearer. Gable and Stewart were out fighting the war. Inside the studio store, however, you could get stockings in a nylon-less world, gas in an energy-poor Los Angeles, and filet mignon in a meat-starved food market.

The Hollywood Hotel made it through the Depression—just barely. The glory days were over though; days in which Valentino tangoed for free at the Thursday tea dance. Warner Brothers was making a film here when the photo was taken, a fraudulent epic with Louella Parsons called, what else, Hollywood Hotel. The film was so dismal that Louella cried when she saw it.

It was 9 p.m., March 29, 1928, and there was no turning back now. The movies had learned to talk!

Of course, the top-secret broadcast from the Hollywood bungalow was only a one shot deal—with Mary, Doug, John Barrymore, Norma Talmadge, D.W. Griffith, Charles Chaplin, and Gloria Swanson appearing for peanuts (less than $50,000 for all of them).

But the significance was all too apparent to the Hollywood press corps: If the seven most important names in silent movies were testing the water in radio; talking pictures were only around the corner.

This trial run was not without its snarls, of course: When Dolores Del Rio tried to sing the title song from her silent movie hit *Ramona*, the sounds came out like this: "Ruh-moan-ah, Aye heer de mishun bells a chime . . . Rah-moan-ah . . ."

To quote a radio reporter for the *New York Times*, "There was no doubt that Dolores did her own singing."

But rumors persist to this day that Norma Talmadge, whose voice was cluttered with a lower Bronx accent, and Gloria Swanson, whose tone was nasal both had voice doubles. (The drawn shades and guards at the dressing room doors did nothing to scotch those rumors.)

Comedian Buster Keaton and one of his custom cars—one of twenty. Keaton, an expert in car-conscious Hollywood, really preferred his yachtlike, thirty-foot land cruiser complete with bunks for six, two drawing rooms, a galley, and observation deck. On top of it all was Keaton in an admiral's uniform. The comedian entrusted construction of the auto to the only firm big enough to do it, the Fifth Avenue Bus Company of New York. No star worth his blown paycheck was immune from carmanship. Even Clark Gable insisted that his Duesenberg be made one foot longer than Gary Cooper's pale green and canary version.

(Far left)
Ramon Novarro had the looks to inherit Valentino's Latin-lover mantle after the Sheik died. He was the movies' first "Ben-Hur" carried the sword as "Scaramouche," and dashed around in a six-inch loin cloth as "The Pagan."

(Left)
They said Thelma Todd had everything—talent, beauty, and even that quality unheard of in the movie capital, a sense of humor. She was only thirty when they found her, dressed in an evening gown and slumped over in her car. Since she had left friends after a party the same night in 1935, police hesitated to rule it a suicide. But then they hesitated to rule it a murder or that catch-all, "an accidental death." "Somebody knew more than they were saying," said Louella Parsons, who always felt that Miss Todd had been murdered.

Mae West the year she broke into the movies—1932. A spiteful Louella Parsons greeted her arrival with the description: "Newcomer Mae West is fat, fair and I don't know how near forty." The snipe was guessing: but Mae was exactly forty the day she reported on the set to make Night After Night. A year later nobody in town was laughing when Mae's pictures—made for a song and written by her—virtually saved Paramount from bankruptcy.

Gilda Gray, with a couple of flower petals covering her breasts and a scrawny grass skirt covering her hips, dances the shimmy to radio music for a magazine advertisement. It's easy to see why it never saw print. The star of an exploitive film, The Devil Dancer, 1928, Miss Gray, in actuality Marianna Michalska of Krakow, Poland, could not parlay her one-dimensional talent into a career. She sang "I Wish I Could Shimmy Like My Sister Kate," over and over and over again.

As the broadcast went out on the fledgling radio networks, moguls all across Hollywood grabbed for either strong spirits or antacid pills.

Every mogul, that is, but Jack Warner, whose studio, a year earlier, had presented the world with the first true sound movie—*The Jazz Singer,* in which Al Jolson uttered the now legendary words, "You ain't heard nothin' yet."

The gamble for Warner Brothers was not as great as it would have been for most of the other studios had they been the first to make a talkie. Warners was still considered to be a second-rate film company whose biggest star, John Barrymore, could obviously talk and whose second biggest star, Rin-Tin-Tin, didn't need to.

"When I saw those lines around the block to see *The Jazz Singer,* I felt that the silent era was over," says Lillian Gish. "What saddened me is that nobody, not one director, not one producer, tried to salvage the beauty of the silent era."

But Hollywood hardly had time for regrets. The moguls—the men who had literally been rag merchants, nuts and bolts dealers, and carnival barkers only fifteen years earlier—were scared.

After a decade of nonstop growth, movie profits in 1926 had dipped for the first time, and sound did it—sound from radio sets that could be put together from fifty cents worth of parts from the corner hardware store.

The price of a movie ticket had soared to the inflationary level of twenty cents. And radio was free. The movie men offered free dishes, live dog acts, second-rate Ziegfeld girls—anything to lure the ticket buyers away from their radio sets.

Nothing worked.

"The whole world became obsessed with sound—any kind of sound," said MGM's whiz kid, Irving Thalberg. The movies were now the old kid on the block.

Radio, the big noise that would become a chasm between the mellow, silent days of Hollywood and the hysteria of the talkies, had grown even faster than the movies had done in their first decade.

The first station had only gone on the air November 2, 1920 (KDKA in Pittsburgh), but by 1922 there were already 564 broadcasting stations. And by 1926 NBC was broadcasting coast to coast and charging $600 a minute for advertising, bringing the infant company $15 million in ad revenue alone in its first year.

It all happened so quickly that NBC didn't have time to find a permanent home for its fast growing Hollywood operation. So the network simply rented the RKO commissary each afternoon for five hours. "It was unbelievable," says Rudy Vallee, one of radio's first three superstars (with Fannie Brice and Eddie Cantor). "We waited until 2:30 when all the movie crews had finished eating and gone back to the sets. Then, while the kitchen crew was still cleaning up we started the warm-ups and went on the air about the time the sound stages were closing."

This wall of sound hit the movies and Hollywood with a crashing body blow—both culturally and economically.

Virtually everyone in Hollywood knew the name Sid Grauman, but only a very few knew what the mastershowman of Hollywood movie palaces looked like. Grauman, left, poses with composer Victor Young.

(Left)
The MGM commissary had world-famous food and a rarified clientele, which meant very little to Joan Crawford, who starved to maintain her luminous-eyed look. The steak and muffins belong to her table partner; Crawford is having her usual soda crackers with mustard and a coddled egg, no butter, no salt. Thirty years later Joan told movie columnist Dorothy Manners, over enchiladas and chili, that her diet made her sad and neurotic for years. "Was it worth it?" Perhaps not, said Crawford.

(Far left)
Mae Murray was one of Hollywood's great natural resources, a beauty of rare cast. Millions of girls imitated her bee-stung lips and her ochre-lidded eyes. Miss Murray made one mistake; she married a tin-horn prince who carried her to a chateau in France. Louis B. Mayer took the move as a slight. So when she came to his office pleading and broke he gave her a flimsy cameo in a Marion Davies movie, allegedly telling directors to make her "look bad and then toss her out."

Even the fabulous paychecks taken home by movie stars (the highest paychecks in American history) paled in comparison to the radio loot. For instance, Chaplin was pulling in $10,000 a week in 1928; Clara Bow got $5,000 and Valentino was the first star to take home $15,000. But radio paid Eddie Cantor $100 a minute and Paul Whiteman $5,000 an hour.

So it was no wonder that Rudy Vallee told a Hollywood studio: "Sure, I'll make a picture—if you can afford me."

Suddenly motion picture economics seemed so complicated, and radio profits seemed so simple. With no effort at all radio could broadcast directly from the stage of a Ziegfeld Follies' opening night with Ruth Etting, Helen Morgan, and Jimmy Durante all on the bill with a singing horse and Singer's Midgets.

So the collective economy of general Hollywoodland, which now included Culver City, Burbank, Santa Monica, and even Laguna, seemed as shaky as the fault lines on which its buildings rested.

And what buildings they had become!

Leering gargoyles stared down from Hollywood Boulevard sky-

Boyish Walt Disney caught with the goods: Mickey Mouse and his forerunner, a family of Kangaroos. Both Disney and Mickey would go on to become one of America's most gifted and enduring success stories.

Hollywood's gift to Hitler, Emil Jannings, who rushed back to Nazi Germany after Americans made him a star. (And incidentally gave him the best actor Oscar.) Jannings, who remained in Europe during World War II, never made a comeback and died of a heart attack in 1950.

scrapers; Babylonian satyrs held up the rooftops of the movie palaces, and Grauman's Chinese Theatre loomed flamboyantly into the air like the bad dream of a Peking emperor on psychedelics.

During the last great decade of the silent film, architects and builders had followed the pied piper's call of movie art directors. Doug Fairbanks built his Robin Hood Castle; ersatz palaces and turreted bungalows quickly showed up in the Hollywood Hills. When D.W. Griffith built his four-story set for *Intolerance,* Babylonian architecture suddenly became the rage—resulting even in a tire factory built like a palazzo on the Euphrates.

Seven hotels, nine office buildings, a thousand bungalows, untold apartment houses, and a scatter of incredible mansions perhaps unequalled in the history of American architecture covered the landscape.

No movie star worth his million dollars a year in 1925 wanted a house when he could have a castle.

"You have to realize that most movie stars and producers, for that matter, were only one step out of the lower-middle-class districts of Europe," said scriptwriter Anita Loos. "So the very height for them would be a castle. And it had to look like it was right out of a fairy story."

Valentino, Barrymore, and Pola Negri all had their castles and spent fortunes furnishing them. Some of the more stingy stars furnished their living rooms with "play" furniture built from paper in the studio art departments. "After all," said Clara Bow. "This is all for show anyway—nobody would want to live in a place like this."

Ramon Novarro even coaxed MGM set designer Cedric Gibbons into decorating his Lloyd Wright house—all in black fur and silver, and he felt that it was so successful that his dinner guests were commanded to wear only black, white, and silver—down to the shoes and handbags. Perhaps the surprising thing is that all of them complied . . . even Louis B. Mayer.

There was plenty to spend on frills in the free-swinging economy of the early talkies when ten stars paid $100,000 a year in income taxes alone. (Doug Fairbanks, Sr., Will Rogers, Harold Lloyd, Norma Shearer, Greta Garbo, Marion Davies, Ann Harding, Constance Bennett, Richard Barthelmess, and Janet Gaynor.)

Later Connie Bennett would say: "I don't know how much money we had to spend in those days—I do know that we spent it all."

In 1931, when more than a dozen silent superstars watched their salaries plunge to nothing, the Hollywood Chamber of Commerce erected a sign near Hollywood and Vine: "Don't Wait for the Good Times—SPEND NOW, and keep business alive."

Garland with Liza on the set of Words and Music. *She was on hiatus when Louis B. Mayer offered her $50,000 to play herself and sing one number to help salvage Mickey's floundering bio of Rodgers and Hart. There was a roar from technicians when the rushes were shown. And Mayer gave her another $50,000 to sing a second song, "Johnny One Note."*

(Below left)
Stardom came early for Judy Garland, too early. Before her small body had time to burn off its "baby fat" and she had learned to deal with a natural tendency to gain weight, MGM executives saw fit to protect their investment in her enormous talent by making weight-loss easy . . . with pills, and a diet that was constantly under scrutiny. As a young teenager in the MGM commissary, she obediently nibbled on steak and learned lines. In the long run, the battle to stay slim cost her her life. Ironically, while almost all of her recorded songs survive, she attained her real immortality in films as a slightly rounded teenager in The Wizard of Oz.

In that year Tom Mix, the cowboy hero, spent a half million bucks on a Beverly Hills mansion, paid back taxes in the amount of $574,000, doled out $18,000 a year on servants, signed a check for $12,000 for his fan mail answering service, and paid out $1,000 for white sombreros. Tom Mix was one of the lucky ones; nobody particularly cared if he could talk well or not. He could shoot straight and mount a galloping horse—that was enough.

Most silent film stars weren't that fortunate.

"It had been a severe shock to see this man (Jolson) open his mouth and hear the voice come out of it—a once in a lifetime experience," said Frank Capra. "Suddenly even the phone books were full of ads that said, 'Train your voice for the talkies.' It was Hollywood's first great panic."

Buddy Rogers, who was later to marry Mary Pickford and eventually inherit Pickfair, said, "Everybody was scared. Could we make it in talking pictures? Each day they took another star into a special sound stage and kept him there for hours."

Rogers and the other stars sat out on the curb all afternoon waiting for a verdict. Suddenly the door to the sound stage would burst open. And a boy would scream: "Harold Lloyd has a voice! Lloyd can talk."

Colleen Moore, who was number one at the box office in 1928 when talkies came in, was one of the many who was sent downtown to one of the famed and ancient stage ladies brought out to teach movie stars how to talk.

"So I went to this famous, famous lady. I arrived for my first lesson. And I looked like a care package . . . I was very young."

The antique stage actress looked down at Colleen Moore through her pince-nez. "YOU are Colleen Moore? Do they really pay you $10,000 a week?"

Moore looked up at her. "No, ma'm, they pay me $12,000."

The actress stayed closeted with the voice teacher for two hours . . . spending all her time learning to say the word "mother." The next week she learned to say "father." After three weeks studio boss Jesse Lasky told her: "At this rate we'll be out a million dollars before you learn to say a full sentence."

Some stars listened to the frightening echo of their own voices and gave up without a fight; Pola Negri and Academy Award winner Emil Jannings both went back to Germany without ever taking a sound test. The *London Daily Mirror* ran a headline above their pictures: "No Spik."

Within six months after *The Jazz Singer* premièred, Hollywood was ruled by sound technicians. Men who had been Marconi operators on the night freighter to Borneo were suddenly king of the studio roosts. "All of the sound geniuses saw it as their chance to take over Hollywood," says director George Cukor. "It was horrible."

(Above)
The smile on pretty-boy Robert Taylor's face is real. Taylor, like everyone else at MGM, truly liked Jean Harlow, the only real "good guy" on the MGM lot of the thirties. Garbo and Shearer even liked her. Joan Crawford couldn't even find it in her heart to be jealous of "The Baby," as they called her.

(Top)
Cary Grant takes home movies of Harlow with Franchot Tone, about to be Crawford's newest love. The year was 1935, and the film was Suzy, *in which the blonde bombshell sang and danced.*

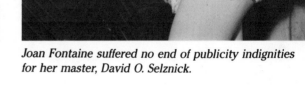

With her hand on Gable's knee and a director's protective arm on her shoulder, Harlow smiles for the still photographer. (At far right is Wallace Beery.) The star is wearing her famous "seven shades of white," a costumer's trick that gave Jean a special glossy look.

Joan Fontaine suffered no end of publicity indignities for her master, David O. Selznick.

A tyranny of noise ruled Hollywood.

Fan magazine legend would later portray dozens of silent stars as tragic victims of sound—stars like super-lover John Gilbert caught up in a web of his own high-pitched tones.

The truth is that few of the silent greats (including Gilbert) were ruined by their own echoes.

Two ten-year studies of the late silent era (By Kevin Brownlow for his book *Hollywood—The Pioneers* and Alexander Walker for *Shattered Silents*) have shown that only a few of the stars (including Norma Talmadge, William Haines, and Vilma Banky) were actually destroyed by their voices.

Sound was just the excuse Louis B. Mayer used to drop both John Gilbert and Francis X. Bushman after social skirmishes between them and the studio chief. (Gilbert reportedly socked Mayer in a mansion restroom when Mayer told him: "Don't marry Garbo—just go to bed with her.")

Clara Bow was rushed into one sound turkey after another; Gloria Swanson made a disaster with her then mentor Joseph Kennedy; Janet Gaynor and Marion Davies were showing their age.

The collapse of some of these careers would reach Greek tragedy proportions and would usher in the "studio system," in which actors were regarded as chattel—to be pampered or thrown to the lions as the studio bosses saw fit.

The destruction of John Gilbert and his early death is the clas-

sic example.

From the day in 1928 when Mayer told Gilbert in the restroom, "I'll break you," Gilbert was living only on borrowed mercy from Thalberg, who protected him, and from Garbo, who used her clout to prop him up.

A year after the silent screen lover signed a $1.5 million contract with MGM (over Mayer's veto), Gilbert was pushed into the now infamous film, *His Glorious Night.* The dialogue was so inane—with Gilbert saying "I love you, I love you" over and over again—and the direction so weak, that audiences laughed openly through each display of passion.

A popular Hollywood wives' tale has Mayer turning up the sound on the film's track in a deliberate attempt to destroy Jack Gilbert. But in the late 1970s Kevin Brownlow, preparing a British TV series on the silents, had *His Glorious Night* screened for a panel of sound technicians. "The technicians told us that Gilbert could not have been incorrectly recorded without affecting the other players in the same scene," says Brownlow. "But the script was appalling and Gilbert's enunciation painful. If only he had been encouraged to relax. . . ."

The creative assassination of Gilbert was a sign that the studios intended to use the sound era as a lever to reduce stars, artists, and writers into chattel who owed feudal dues to the front office.

"Within two years," says Cecil B. De Mille, "our little old Hollywood was gone, and in its place stood a fair, new city, talking a new language, having different manners and customs—a more terrifying city

Robert Young ("Marcus Welby"), Franchot Tone, and Ronald Reagan's best friend Robert Taylor on the set of Three Comrades, which starred them with the fragile Margaret Sullivan. The trio is dashing and picture-postcard handsome on the surface, but they were all tormented with their own demons. Taylor would later turn in his friends during the black-list period, Young battled booze, Tone died bitter and alone.

Crawford in 1949, posed on the lawn of her Brentwood mansion with her matching poodles and matching shoes, belt, blouse, and hair ribbon. A fan took this photo; by that time Joan had put her fans to work answering fan mail, addressing Christmas cards, and signing autographs.

Deanna Durbin—the little girl L.B. Mayer really wanted when he was stuck with Judy Garland. He had seen a short called "Every Sunday" and told his assistant: "Sign up that singer—the flat one." (Durbin's voice was a wee bit flat.) The anxious young man thought Mayer said "the fat one." And signed up Garland, letting Durbin go to Universal where her movies brought in a cool hundred million in ten years.

The most closely guarded movie stills in Hollywood were the costume and Technicolor tests made at the beginning of every film. There was good reason—the stars were shown naked of the makeup, lighting, and nip and tuck tricks that made the stars not only larger than life but more perfect than thou. Every now and then a shot would be bribed off the lot and do unlimited damage. A vignette of four unreleased tests shows four of the biggest stars without their studio armor.

Liz Taylor with unfitted costume, uncoiffed hair, and poor stance in test for Father of the Bride.

Gable, a bit paunchy and looking smaller than life, in the test for Mogambo. (MGM was to let even the King go shortly after this film).

Van Johnson, coming off rather well in college dress—probably Mother Was A Freshman.

And Bob Walker, the star deserted by Jennifer Jones for David Selznick, showing the signs of his battle with booze and pills. Note, he's testing for the part of Jerome Kern in Till The Clouds Roll By. And this is the "young makeup."

full of strange faces, less friendly, more businesslike, twice as populous. And much more cruel."

Sound killed forever the carefree, festive atmosphere of moviemaking.

Movie historian Alexander Walker, film critic for the *London Evening Standard,* said: "The talkie era imposed a form of servitude on the industry for which glamour was the only camouflage and fame the only adequate consolation."

Talkies took twice as long to make and demanded nerves of steel and the patience of Job from the actors, bringing to Hollywood a more abrasive breed of stars—Bette Davis, Jean Harlow, James Cagney, Joan Crawford, Fred Astaire, and Ginger Rogers.

The studio manufactured names and identities for its star products and then sent them out in packets of eight-by-ten glossies. Claudette Cauchoin became Claudette Colbert, Frances Gumm became Judy Garland, Betty Perske became Lauren Bacall. Marion Morrison became John Wayne; Reginald Truscott-Jones became Ray Milland. . . .

To match their new names, new hair color, new teeth, and—sometimes—new faces, the fan magazines, gossip columnists, and studio PR men had to invent a glittering and glamorous nightlife to match.

(Above)
An early movie starlet emerging from a giant cake (top left), was typical of the nightly antics at the Coconut Grove— Hollywood's major watering place in the 20s and 30s. Gable and Lombard met here; Harlow and Paul Bern met here; and it was also the battleground of the celebrated feuds between Hedda Hopper and Louella Parsons. The palm trees were fake naturally, fashioned by a set decorator, and rabbit skin monkeys, similarly fashioned, dropped down nightly at midnight.

Betty Grable, who ten years later succeeded Connie Bennett as the highest paid woman in America, dances with former child star Jackie Coogan, just before she hit it really big as a pinup and dancing star. Nobody argued that Grable was the "10" of the forties.

I'm singing Xmas carols
Atop the garden wall.
My dog however seems to feel
It isn't good at all.

Rudy Vallee and one of his cute Christmas cards of the thirties. The dog's hiding his face, and so did his neighbors several decades later when the Vagabond Lover pressured them to rename his street, "Rue de Vallee." When they turned thumbs down, Rudy put up the sign anyway over his megaphone mail box, both he and it an enduring Hollywood fixture atop Mulholland Drive.

(Above)
Irving Thalberg and his wife, Norma Shearer, after a ping pong match at their ocean mansion in Santa Monica. Thalberg was to die in 1936, but long after he had made her a star. Here, in 1930, Thalberg was at the peak of his power. Later, Thalberg was to bear the brunt or criticism of building Norma's career on the bones of other Metro stars. In fact, William Randolph Hearst pulled Marion Davies off the Metro lot because Thalberg refused to star Miss Davies in Marie Antoinette *and* The Barrets of Wimpole Street, *projects he was saving for Norma. After Thalberg's death, Shearer was hounded by MGM's Louis B. Mayer.*

A careless glance at the Sunday rotogravure sections in the 1930s and 1940s (in almost any city) would lead you to believe that stars spent a few hours a day making movies—spending the rest of the time motoring from one party to another; from one gay nightspot to another; from one romantic dalliance to another—altogether an entirely erroneous picture of movie stardom. (Which almost always required stars to work twelve hours a day.)

Because a lively backdrop was needed for these flights of fanciful publicity, the institution known as the Sunset Strip was born: that ribbon of nightclubs and restaurants on a strip of land squeezed between the cities of Los Angeles and Beverly Hills.

From the intimacy of the Sheherezade, near Doheny Drive, where the Luckman Building now stands, to the Garden of Allah at Crescent Heights Boulevard, where Great Western Savings is now, the brightest stars and most powerful movie moguls dined, drank, danced, and made the gossip columns in the dozens of clubs and cafes lining both sides of the boulevard.

An aerial view of the Hollywood studios of Mary Pickford and Douglas Fairbanks showing (center), the set of Fairbanks' The Thief of Bagdad, *1923.*

Earl Carroll's on Sunset Boulevard in Hollywood was one of the more pretentious supper clubs which catered more to tourists hoping to catch a glimpse of movie stars than the stars themselves. It was owned and hosted initially by Carroll himself, who had produced "Earl Carroll's Vanities" on Broadway in New York, and lived extravagantly on both coasts, usually surrounded by his own beautiful showgirls. In 1929 however, on a flight from Philadelphia, he and his real love, the beautiful Beryl Wallace, perished together. The club, much later, became Hollywood's Aquarius Theater, where the smash musical of the sixties, Hair, made its debut.

Ciro's, the top superstar water hole for three decades, doesn't look so hot here in the mid-afternoon. After the sun set, the stars rushed in, if only to have their pics snapped and then rush off to curlers and cold cream before the early morning call. Hollywood purists insist that the club's present reincarnation as the Comedy Store is a comedown. But Robin Williams, Steve Martin, and Lily Tomlin all emerged there. Potent stuff of the seventies.

The famous Trocadero, one of a trio of nightclubs on the Sunset Strip which could be depended upon to attract the post-première crowds of movie stars and an even larger coterie of fans. Originally a popular eatery known as La Boheme, it was located at 8610 Sunset Boulevard, now the address of a big hole almost adjacent to what used to be the Playboy Club and is now Hollywood executive offices for Playboy Enterprises. During the war years, apart from the big bands and headliner acts, like Hazel Scott or Mary Lou Williams, the most popular late-night spot at the Troc was the King Cole Room, where King Cole and his trio frequently played to the "in" group long past midnight, official curfew-time for all bars and nightclubs during World War II.

Wolff's Lair, the prototype Hollywood castle of 1925, was named after a studio art director turned developer. The man built it into an island of small chateaux in the sky, overlooking Beachwood Canyon and Lake Hollywood. It included a heart-shaped pool, a tiny turret built for a pet Gibbon, and the Tiffany half moon that lights the terrace. It has come down almost intact and is now the home of author and realtor Bob Crane.

A natty Rudolph Valentino, his dog, and his car (a 1925 French Voisin) pose before his home in Whitley Heights, near the Hollywood Bowl. This home was never known as Falcon's Lair, although Rudy and his wife, Natasha Rambova, did own it and live in it, however briefly. The real Falcon's Lair, extravagantly palatial, was a sprawling Mediterranean-style hilltop mansion centered on eight acres in Benedict Canyon above Beverly Hills. After Valentino's death (August 23, 1926) the Whitley Heights house and its surrounding acreage were sold for $5,000. Complete destruction followed a few years later to make room for the Hollywood Freeway. Falcon's Lair, first sold in the early thirties for $18,000. Then, refurbished, it was resold by its private owner for about $200,000, and the land was ultimately subdivided. It is now worth several million. So goes Hollywood and Beverly Hills real estate.

This house on Laurel Canyon was built "overnight" for a visit of the Prince of Wales to Hollywood in the twenties. Set designers and builders loaned from four studios helped erect it—planting more than 1,000 fully grown flowers, trees, and shrubs within three days. This was all in vain. The prince never stayed in the house; never even saw it. Instead, he turned thumbs down on the ostentation of the movie city and went to stay in a blueblood's mansion on Coronado Island near San Diego. It was there that he met Wallace Warfield Simpson— starting a romance that was to topple him off the throne.

(Right)
Chateau Trianon, the twenty-nine-unit apartment building which has dominated the corner of Serrano and Loma Linda avenues in Hollywood since 1929 when, we are told, it was built by film-stars Mary Pickford and Douglas Fairbanks partially as an investment and partly to serve as an interim home while Pickfair was under construction.

The Hollywood white way after the coming of radio—which suddenly reactivated downtown Hollywood, making it the center of worldwide radio which doubled the gross income of the city. Moviemen laughed when NBC started its West Coast studio in the commissary of the RKO Film Studio. Within five years, NBC would pay stars double their movie takehome—slowly luring them to a newer, greener pasture.

Al Jolson, Lionel Barrymore, and singer Dixie Lee (later Mrs. Bing Crosby) in an early NBC radio broadcast in the commissary at RKO which served, after hours, as NBC West Coast. Note Jolson's relaxed tan; radio paid him enough to let him work half the time and relax in Palm Springs.

Bing Crosby on banjo and "Ike" the singing coyote harmonizing. The coyote-sized mike was supplied especially for the pup by NBC who would use a coyote and anything else to break into the radio big-time—an honor already afforded CBS.

Among the most famous, perhaps, were Mocambo, which began as Club Versailles, and the Trocadero, an offshoot of the original La Boheme, both on the south side of Sunset where empty lots and the Playboy Building are today. Although interiors of the Troc are immortalized in the original *Star is Born* production starring Janet Gaynor and Frederic March, two steps leading nowhere from the corner of its one-time entrance are all that remain of it today.

Farther east, on the north side of Sunset, film-director Preston Sturgis bought the old Hollywood Wedding Chapel and converted it into the Players Club, where everybody who was anybody even remotely connected with films or the movie press was bound to show up sometime during the week for cocktails, lunch, or dinner. Today, that glamorous retreat from the realities of World War II is the Imperial Gardens, a Japanese restaurant.

Despite meat and gas rationing, chauffeured limousines discharged their cargoes of stars at the Cock 'n Bull, where prime rib was somehow available, and where the two-fisted drinkers of the industry learned to drink Moscow Mules, a Cock 'n Bull vodka concoction, and cope with wartime "Scotch-type whisky." Across the street, at 9157 Sunset, *Time,* Inc. established its first Los Angeles Editorial Bureau, conveniently close to another dimly-lighted bar and restaurant named Scandia, in easy walking distance eastward on the same side of the street.

There were other "in" places along the strip where anyone in search of gaiety could be relatively sure of finding it. One such place was

It's rain folks—Mary Kathleen Moore and Carlton Morse cook up the sound effects for an early NBC radio show. With water, cellophane, sand, and wooden hammers, early technicians could create the entire universe of sound.

Club Gala, semi-concealed inside and out in a portion of the Baronnes d'Erlanger's spacious Spanish home at Sunset Boulevard and Horn Avenue, now an Armenian restaurant.

Across the boulevard on Holloway, just a few feet east of where it merges into Sunset, pianologist Bruz Fletcher had his own coterie of admirers at the Bali, another intimate club whose sophisticated entertainment tended to attract more men than women. Ironically, years later what had once been Club Bali became a massage parlor, now defunct!

On the north side of Sunset, near Sunset Plaza, the Club International (where Cyrano's is today) featured a handsome male impersonator who appeared to be far more attractive to women than to men.

At Ciro's and Mocambo, too, males and females unaccompanied by at least one member of the opposite sex were discouraged from admittance, ostensibly to herd off hustlers. As a result, it was common practice for one woman to arrive with three or more male escorts, and one man to enter the bar with more than one pretty girl in tow. Once inside, it was everyone for himself. Rarely did the same group depart intact.

Nearly every club had its big-name entertainers. At the Troc, the King Cole Trio had its own room. Black pianist Hazel Scott swept into Mocambo, dragging a luxuriously long white fox scarf behind her, to play "boogie" on the Steinway Grand. Xavier Cugat and his band performed at Ciro's; Edie and Rack played piano and sang Dwight Fiske material at the Gala, while a couple of blocks away, at Chez Boheme (where Little Shanghai is today) Ray Bourbon queened it over every other entertainer, in his own sardonic way.

Near Harper Avenue, in the hills immediately above Sunset, Hollywood's great and near-great moved to the cry of the croupier at the Clover Club, before and after Prohibition had been repealed.

Before the Hollywood press agents ran out of time in the 1960s, the Strip had become so synonymous with glamour that it ranked with streets in Paris, Rome, and London as centers of excitement.

In truth, nightclubs like Ciro's, Mocambo, and the Trocadero were as important as "sets" for Hollywood as the sound stages at Paramount or MGM. A limo would pick up, for instance, Loretta Young and George Brent, deposit them at the Trocadero just long enough for Hymie Frank to take a picture, and then rush them back to the studio.

There, they would take off the studio tuxedo and the gown from the costume department before they headed home to learn their lines for the 7 a.m. call.

This dishonest facade eventually reached such a point by 1953

Conrad Nagel finally turned to radio to revive his career—after studios tried without success to make him the first romantic idol in the talkie era. They crammed him into a Hussar's uniform to kiss Marion Davies, decked him out as a 1905 Navy lieutenant for a Japanese idyll, put him in white tights and let him squirm on a couch full of Napoleonic ladies, and gave him a tailor-made tux to star as the heartthrob of Elinor Glynn's Three Weeks. *The kisses, however, turned to laughter. And it was radio that revived his power.*

Thomas Freebairn-Smith, an early-day matinee idol of radio, broadcasts live at the dedication of the Los Angeles Federal Building. As radio went into every American home, people avoided theaters, bringing to Hollywood its first panic.

This crowd for a "man on the street" broadcast shows some of the excitement of impromptu shows . . . it was clearly everyman's medium, the forerunner of television. The average radio show earned six times the average movie—investment dollar for investment dollar.

A castle radio built, the soaring KFAC towers on the edge of Hollywood—this lesson in affluence was not lost on the movies.

138

(Above right)
Radio shows wooed the biggest names in Hollywood as participants in network specials beamed from local NBC and CBS studios at Sunset Boulevard and Vine Street and ABC network headquarters around the corner on Vine. Here, in January 1936, Cecil B. De Mille and Bing Crosby traded barbs on NBC, two years after De Mille had produced Cleopatra, *the first in his long series of historical films. Born August 21, 1881, De Mille had directed seventy films, from* The Squaw Man *(1913) to* The Ten Commandments *(1956) before he died in his Hollywood hills home at 2010 De Mille Drive on January 21, 1959. His original* Ten Commandments *premièred at Grauman's Egyptian Theatre December 4, 1923. In 1941, on his sixtieth birthday, his hand-and-footprints were embedded in concrete at Grauman's Chinese Theatre, where his spectacular* King of Kings *had premièred in April 1927.*

(Above left)
Bob Hope on an early radio show in downtown Hollywood.

Silent comedienne Louise Fazenda turns traitor to the movies in a promotion for a radio show. Fazenda, wife of producer Hal Wallis, was the unbeatable queen of the two-reel comedy and one of the films' finest character actresses.

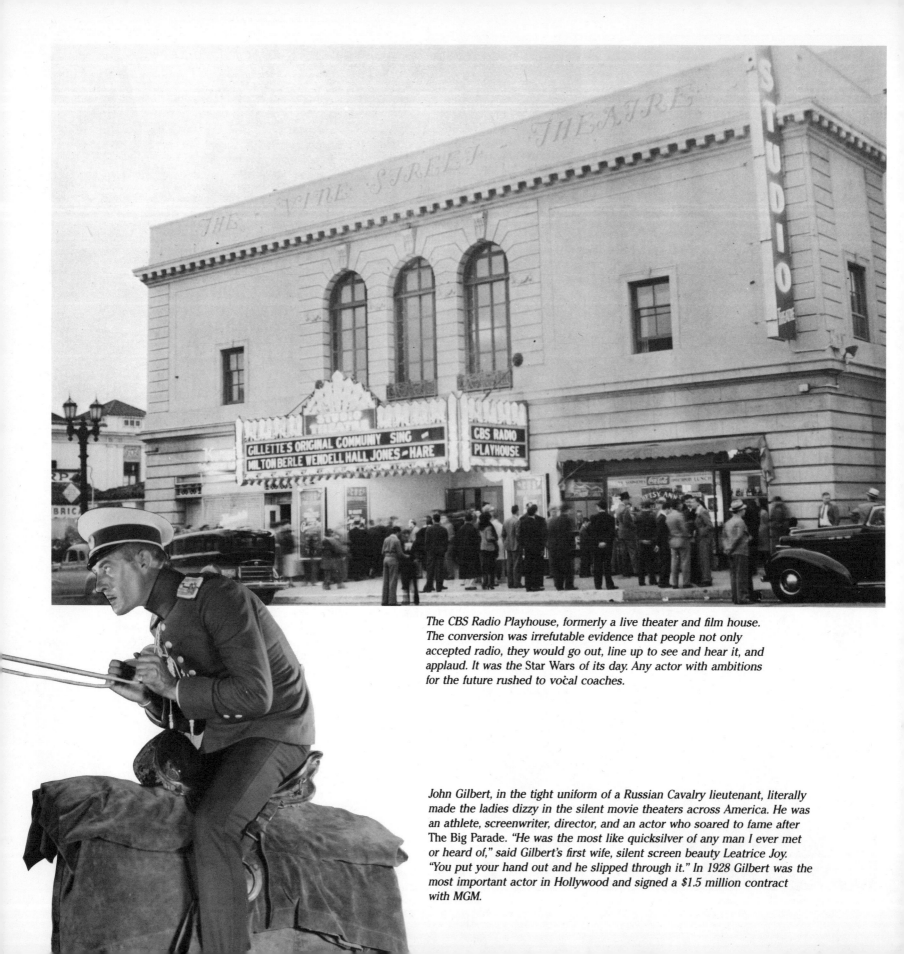

The CBS Radio Playhouse, formerly a live theater and film house. The conversion was irrefutable evidence that people not only accepted radio, they would go out, line up to see and hear it, and applaud. It was the Star Wars of its day. Any actor with ambitions for the future rushed to vocal coaches.

John Gilbert, in the tight uniform of a Russian Cavalry lieutenant, literally made the ladies dizzy in the silent movie theaters across America. He was an athlete, screenwriter, director, and an actor who soared to fame after The Big Parade. "He was the most like quicksilver of any man I ever met or heard of," said Gilbert's first wife, silent screen beauty Leatrice Joy. "You put your hand out and he slipped through it." In 1928 Gilbert was the most important actor in Hollywood and signed a $1.5 million contract with MGM.

Another bride, another groom. Another Hollywood honeymoon: Constance Bennett, the highest paid woman in America, and her husband (inherited from Gloria Swanson), Henri, Marquis de la Falaise de la Coudray, immediately after their wedding in Beverly Hills. Neither marriage lasted, but Swanson and Bennett were, at least, Marquises for a day—a feat that forever ensured their welcomes at title-conscious Pickfair.

Leo Carillo in the annual Santa Claus Lane Parade down Hollywood Boulevard. The parade is one of the few Hollywood institutions still alive today.

Other stars were going down for the count as the thirties ended, but Gable put on a Maurice Chevalier hat, lifted an Astaire cane— singing and dancing to "Puttin' On The Ritz" in Idiot's Delight opposite Norma Shearer. When the film was one month into the theaters an avalanche of mail poured in threatening MGM for so ill using the king. They never made that mistake again. The scene, rescued for That's Entertainment in 1974, brought down the house.

Mickey Rooney, here as Puck in A Midsummer Night's Dream, became Judy Garland's co-star and soul mate for twenty years. Mickey didn't get hooked on pills as did Judy; he just found himself misused and discarded when he grew out of his "cute" period.

SUNSET LIMITED

Dolores Del Rio, smothered in flowers, embarks from Pasadena on the private Sunset Limited car of the old Santa Fe Super Chief—which whisked the stars in luxury to Chicago in only 2½ days. Miss Del Rio traveled with thirty-two pieces of luggage, a staff of six (including masseur), and two studio execs to handle her publicity and arrival plans.

that a day of work for Marilyn Monroe in 1953 would fit this schedule: 5 a.m.—Twentieth Century-Fox limo picks up Marilyn at the Beverly Hills Hotel. 5:30 a.m.—makeup at Twentieth Century-Fox. 8 a.m.—first call, sound stage seven, *How To Marry A Millionaire.* 6 p.m.—last take, sound stage seven. 6:30 p.m.—Marilyn reports to makeup for a shampoo, comb, and set. 7 p.m.—Marilyn is fitted by Fox costume department with a gold lamé evening gown, a white ermine coat, and diamond earrings. 8 p.m.—studio limousine drops Marilyn at the front entrance to Grauman's Chinese Theatre, she goes in the front, comes out the side and is picked up on Hollywood Boulevard by the chauffeur. 9 p.m.— Marilyn is dropped at the entrance to Mocambo—exiting at 10:30 p.m. Midnight—Marilyn is returned to makeup, sheds the dress, the jewels, the furs—leaves for home in a taxi and wearing levis and Joe Di Maggio's old sweatshirt.

VI THE WAR, HOLLYWOOD PATRIOTISM, AND THE FINAL GREAT YEARS

World War II as MGM wanted it to be—a $200,000 romp in hand-tailored sailor suits and gold lamé gowns. The movie was 1954's Hit The Deck, *with, from left: Jane Powell, Vic Damone, Ann Miller, Tony Martin, Debbie Reynolds, and Russ Tamblyn.*

Gable called Carole Lombard "Ma" from the moment of their wedding in Kingman, Arizona—the only town in which they were safe from an already suspicious press. (Gable had to hide in the rumble seat while Lombard without makeup and in jeans and pigtails stopped for gas and food.)

Louella Parsons was in the middle of a sentence—surrounded by superstars—when a tall chauffeur in tails grabbed her arm and then whispered something in her ear.

Joan Crawford saw Louella's face go chalk white and heard her sob as she walked toward the door—then she remembered her guests and turned back to Joan: "Joan, it's Carole; her plane crashed."

Crawford grabbed the edge of a marble table and asked, "Does Clark know?" Louella shook her head—"No, not yet." . . . Helping Louella to the car, Crawford leaned over and said, "Well, the war's come home to us now, hasn't it? And I'm afraid this is only the first of our losses."

It was 8 p.m. on Friday, January 16, 1942, and the war had, indeed, come home to Hollywood.

Later that night Joan Crawford sent a telegram to Clark Gable,

The waiting game was a way of life for GIs in World War II, but nowhere did they queue up so patiently and with such anticipation as at the Hollywood Canteen for Servicemen just south of Sunset on Cahuenga Boulevard. Entrance was freely accorded anyone in uniform. A GI's wartime jitters found an exhausting outlet in jitterbugging to the sounds of the most popular big bands of the day. Any GI could talk to, dance with, be served food by Joan Crawford, Marlene Dietrich, Ella Fitzgerald, Janice Paige, Mrs. John Ford, Sybil Brand, Betty Grable, Ingrid Bergman, Hedy Lamarr, Frances Langford, Dorothy Lamour, and hundreds more, who entertained as well. But does anyone know what happened to First Sergeant Carl E.W. Bell from Rising Star, Texas, after he was kissed by Marlene Dietrich because he happened to be the one millionth serviceman to walk through the canteen door?

a man she had been in love with less than ten years earlier. "Clark, I'll be home tonight and any other night this month, if you care to come over and talk."

"Oh, I know that all this sounds so trite and silly," says author Adela Rogers St. Johns. "But Hollywood was a small town. We talked over the back fence—so to speak. Carole Lombard's death was a family death for us. It may have been corny, but that's the way it was. Clark Gable's loss was our loss . . . it was like that."

By the time Carole Lombard's plane crashed into a mountain as the blonde star was coming home from a bond rally, Hollywood was heavily committed to the war effort: John Garfield and Bette Davis had founded the Hollywood Canteen; twenty war propaganda films were before the cameras, and the British colony (Basil Rathbone, Robert Donat, Vivien Leigh, and Bebe Daniels) had long since gone back to London to fight the Germans.

Typically, Hollywood's only real brush with war could have been invented on an MGM sound stage. The date was February 25, 1942, and the fog had moved in early, dampening the atmosphere on a town that was already blacked out each night by 6 p.m. Suddenly, the heavy rumble of anti-aircraft guns caused visible ripples on the plaster-and-paper sets at MGM and Paramount studios.

Dimes never again marched amid such mobs as they "marched" into the first star-studded March of Dimes funding event during the war years of the early forties. Crowds at the intersection of Hollywood and Vine paralyzed traffic, obstructing movement of the Hollywood Boulevard/West Hollywood Red Car loaded with commuters bound for home after a hard day's work downtown.

(Below)
Joan Fontaine getting her volunteer Red Cross Nurse cap after a grueling six months of instruction. Fontaine gave up her night life from 1942–45, making a real effort where many stars only patriotized on film.

Judy Garland, filming a musical number, ran out the back gates of the studio and saw red-and-yellow flashes—like fireworks in the sky. Then a light rain of casing shrapnel—much of it still red hot—pelted the bungalows of Hollywood's flatlands. Later, satirists would call it "The Battle for Hollywood" (part of the inspiration for Stephen Spielberg's $45 million epic, *1941*), but not many people laughed that night. At one point, according to Hollywood historian Bruce Torrence, "People formed into mobs and went beserk. When the blackout wasn't immediately effective, the mobs roamed through downtown Hollywood smashing through store fronts to put out the lights themselves . . . there was real hysteria."

Within thirty days, more than 1,000 stars, technicians, directors, and writers had enlisted—in a growing list that included Clark Gable, Jimmy Stewart, Robert Taylor, Frank Capra, Victor Mature, and Tyrone Power. (Census figures show that seventy-five percent of all Hollywood families had at least one member in uniform—29,000 in all.)

Hollywood Boulevard erupted in a festival atmosphere it would retain until the end of the war—a flush of profits, building, glamour, and excitement that many would call the sunset of Hollywood's golden era. Movie attendance soared to 90,000,000 a week; the box office take jumped from $735,000,000 in 1940 to $1,500,000,000 in 1945; star's salaries climbed to dizzy heights (with Betty Grable, at $800,000 a year, becoming the highest paid woman in American history.

The "Hollywood Style" in clothes, cars, and cafes instantly spread around the world: (Women in Calcutta adopted Veronica Lake's peek-a-boo bangs; matrons in London moved into Spanish bungalows like Joan Crawford's in *Mildred Pierce,* and Alan Ladd's black coupe became the world's most popular bachelor car).

Most film critics and social observers technically date the start of the golden age at 1937 when *Gone With The Wind* began filming at David Selznick's studio in Culver City . . . after a publicity inspired "let's pretend" search across America for just that particular "new face" that would bring Scarlett O'Hara to life. What the press releases failed to say was that Selznick never intended to cast an unknown. In fact, most people feel he never even looked at the thousands of screen tests he ordered. It was just a bit too convenient that he ended up casting a client of his brother Myron—a young English actress named Vivien Leigh.

Selznick's publicity men also failed to say that *Gone With The Wind*'s author Margaret Mitchell burst into gales of laughter when she saw the unrealistic set for Tara, which was only a plywood shell of a plantation. Even the curtains were only wisps of painted silk. "How appropriate," said the author. "A true Hollywood version of the old South; it has no heart."

After 1937 much of Hollywood was like that; all glitter and panache on the outside but soulless in the center. The rock-and-crystal mansions of the great silent stars had become haunted houses; John Barrymore fell back in death agony on his velvet sofa set amidst Parisian antiques; passé comedian Harold Lloyd sat isolated in his huge mansion Greenacres watching reel after reel of his silent comedies and reacting, said a friend, like he was seeing an utterly fascinating stranger on the screen. Valentino was long dead in his tomb—his life bled away by a perforated ulcer which ate into him as he tried, vainly, to live up to his own publicity.

MGM's greatest producer, a wunderkind named Irving Thalberg, died at thirty-seven—worn out by building up the studio he made great.

But the mythmakers kept turning out spun-sugar legends that might evaporate under the magnifying glass of reality. Take the Hollywood Canteen, where the boys in blue and khaki danced with Linda Darnell, shared a cup with Dietrich, or sang along with Alice Faye. Truthfully, Hollywood stars rarely showed up. And then only for show . . . dropping in with their press agents, their photographers and then dashing off to Ciro's or Mocambo without breaking a fingernail. In a reminiscence of the canteen, Betty Alnes wrote: "The big-name people rarely showed up. Oh, there were some loyal regulars. Like Bette Davis, who was president, and was always there. Some of our now famous actresses popped up onstage, hoping to be spotted by agents."

Even the Hollywood social life of the late thirties and early

Rita Hayworth serving pie at the Hollywood Canteen just before she turned the corner to superstardom. Only months after this picture, surgeons raised Hayworth's hairline, makeover wizards took twenty pounds off her, and makeup men worked thirty days to give her a new face. The job was complete by 1942 when a Life *magazine photographer shot her in a silk nightgown on the bed, achieving the second most popular pinup of the war years.*

forties was about as solid as a Christmas display in a window at I. Magnin. Glossy magazines like *Photoplay* and the rotogravure sections in the Hearst papers presented picture-book versions of Tinseltown's 400 such as the blowout Ouida and Basil Rathbone tossed for their eleventh anniversary. They commanded their 250 guests to come as famous bridal couples. And nobody argued. Movie stars who had been slaving in costumes all day peeled off their pancake makeup and climbed into painfully accurate disguise: for instance, the Edward G. Robinsons came as Napoleon and Josephine; Gene Raymond and Jeanette MacDonald as Romeo and Juliet, and Loretta Young, unaccompanied, as Satan.

But it was fake chic. A real socialite, Cornelius Vanderbilt, Jr., satirized all of it in a book he called *Why Fifth Avenue Laughs at Hollywood Society.* "It may have been simply just a case of too much dough," wrote Vanderbilt. "Going to a really 'in' party out in Hollywood is like paying your two-bits in the peanut gallery down on Main and Seventh to watch the greatest show on earth. All about me at the party are the Four Hundred of Picturedom, cellophane-wrapped and pretending to have a good time . . . all simply dreadful."

Underneath all this carefully erected Hollywood chic lurked a long flirtation with the elite of organized crime that stretched back to Al Capone's visit to Hollywood in 1927 when he was welcomed by the studios with wide-open gates. That was the signal for an influx of mobsters who came from Chicago and New York to winter in the film capital. (The arrangement grew so cozy that most of them bunked at the posh Garden of Allah and took their toddies with F. Scott Fitzgerald, Jean Harlow, and Norma Talmadge.)

It was the blue collar workers at the studio, however, who unwittingly brought mob rule into town as a package deal during a ticklish union movement. Willie Bioff and George Browne, who reputedly had underworld ties, had slithered into top power ranks of the International Alliance of Theatrical Stage Employees and Moving Picture Operators (IATSE).

In a series of complicated underworld moves, Bioff and Browne caught the IATSE in a stranglehold, and Hollywood was threatened with a national projectionists strike. A few of the right calls from the mob to the front offices of MGM and other studios and the payoffs flooded in. At first, payments were handed over in cash to Bioff in the bar at the Garden of Allah; later bribes of $100,000 or more—wrapped in brown paper—were deposited with a bellboy at a hotel desk in Manhattan. (The Screen Actor's Guild would, in a rare show of courage, expose the IATSE scandal. But not before Fox exec Joseph Schenck was sent to prison for laundering money for Bioff and the mob.)

So it was only natural when mob kingpin Bugsy Siegel blew into town, setting himself up in several Hollywood hilltop homes and bringing with him his ace lieutenant, Mickey Cohen. This duo would eventually become so cozy with the movie elite that most big-time stars had at least passing contact with the Siegel circle. (Cohen, for example would set up his mother in an ice cream parlor out in Brentwood—with just everyone motoring out on Sundays to sample the pistachio or maple

Original Brown Derby restaurant on Wilshire Boulevard in 1941 attracted tourists and natives alike to ogle filmland's greats. Meanwhile, lest recognition falter, the restaurant provided an inescapably insistent paging service and portable telephones which were hand-carried to celebrities' tables and plugged in with a flourish which lacked only a fanfare of trumpets. More often than not, the page had been rigged by a press agent. There was no one on the other end of the line.

Everybody who was anybody, my dear, lunched at the Derby at least once a week during the most glamorous days of the picture biz. Further, everyone ate Cobb salad, even if it made him sick. It was the "in" thing for lunch. The Derby, for whatever reason, had few true competitors. It was the place to see and be seen.

Otto Preminger, Gene Tierney, and a friend out for the evening at
Hollywood's Mocambo. A cozy evening in exciting Hollywood. Or
was it? Press agents became so adept at ushering stars into the
clubs, messing up a table, photographing a tête-à-tête, and then
getting them out again that the real thing was hard to find. Even

Hedda and Louella printed cozy twosomes nationwide—only to
find out later that it was all a stunt. (Most stars, in reality, had
less than a half hour for such frippery—reporting to the set as
they did at 6 a.m. each of six days a week.

nut. And it was a Cohen lieutenant, Johnny Stompanato, murdered in
the incident involving Lana Turner and her daughter Cheryl).

Movie hostesses, with their policy of invite first, ask questions
later, were well involved with Siegel and Cohen before papers began to
hint at the mob connections. Bugsy dated starlets Wendy Barrie and
Marie McDonald, set up gambling on the coast, and began building Vegas
into a showcase. (In one of his classier efforts, Siegel got control of
Hollywood's largest castle, Castillo del Lago, and turned it into a gambling and hooch parlor.)

A highly illuminating incident described by Cohen indicates the
high level of mob-to-star shoulder rubbing. "On Benny's orders," said
Cohen (Benny was Siegel's preferred name—nobody called him Bugsy
to his face), "I went into this private club and raised the joint. I had the
shotgun on everybody. I was watching this good-looking lady and the
guy with her. Goddamn, she was beautiful. I knew she was a movie
person. But who the hell was she? We got the dough and the jewelry
and we took off."

Two years later—after Cohen had moved higher up the mob
ladder—he was at a party, again in Hollywood, when he looked up and
saw this little "blonde casing me and whispering something to Florabel
Muir, the *New York Daily News* Hollywood columnist."

So Florabel walked over to Cohen: "Mickey, do you remember
that little lady over there?" asked the gossip writer. Cohen said: "Yeah,
that's a movie star."

"That's Betty Grable," Muir answered. "Yeah, you met her before,
you took her jewelry."

In many ways Hollywood stars arm-in-arm with the mob was no
surprise. In its fourth decade the movie capital had become a mix-and-
match society; stars and Nazis (both Pola Negri and Emil Jannings were,
according to some accounts, more than nodding acquaintances of
Hitler); Hollywood and far eastern moguls (Rita Hayworth and Aly Kahn,
Gene Tierney and Aly Kahn, Susan Strasberg and Aly . . .) and Hollywood
and political bosses (Joe Kennedy and paramour Gloria Swanson, Adlai
Stevenson and Lauren Bacall, the Kennedy brothers and just about every

To Juliette "The Indispensable" Paulette Goddard

the screen.

A habit that would continue to plague Hollywood's leading matinee idols involved a number of nubile girls. Publicly, it started with Chaplin, the world's first male superstar—who, long after his tramp was starting to trudge into the sunset, was linked with several of his young protégées. The printer's ink on the Chaplin scandal was barely dry when a bedroom full of teenage bathing beauties descended publicly on Errol Flynn, including two girls who swore on the court Bible that Flynn had lured them onto his yacht and committed rape—statuatory, to be sure, but rape all the same. Or so the girls said. The case was so weak that even the judge laughed. But forever after, Flynn was known by the slogan that appeared during the trial—"In like Flynn."

A lot of it was baloney slung by Errol himself. For instance, the genial swashbuckler once persuaded an accountant at Warner Brothers to prove mathematically that he had bedded down with women "approximately 16,000 to 18,000 times." When Errol wryly presented this prize to his studio boss, Jack L. Warner, the mogul only smiled and sent him back to his sword and tights. But Warner would tell Hedda Hopper: "If Errol had bedded all the girls he said he did and the girls who said THEY did it with him, he would have been dead at twenty-two. (As it was, Flynn died at fifty—a dissipated Riviera expatriate whose features

(Above)
Rita and Frankie presiding over the death of glamour at the première of Pal Joey. *He sang "Lady Is A Tramp" to her; she sang "Bewitched, Bothered and Bewildered"; but a blonde newcomer named Kim Novak sang "My Funny Valentine" off key and stole the show.*

(Above right)
Van Johnson, Zsa Zsa Gabor and Johnny Ray at Ciro's during the nightclub years.

(Above left)
Paulette Goddard, a Ziegfeld Girl at fourteen, became Hollywood's most poignant also-ran, coming within a contract inch of playing Scarlett O'Hara in Gone With the Wind, *but losing out because she arrogantly turned down David O. Selznick's demand that she prove her marriage to Charles Chaplin. Charlie, who courted her when she was nineteen, gave her a startling debut by starring her opposite him in* Modern Times. *She ended up playing in films like* Babes In Bagdad *and* The Sins of Jezebel.

153

The pinup photo—a Hollywood institution literally inseparable from the last golden decade of the movies—the forties. "No one who was not around at the time can really understand the power that suddenly accrued to the star lucky enough to become a wartime pinup," said public relations wizard Henry Rogers, who founded Rogers and Cowan—on the strength of a pinup he secured for his first bonafide client, Rita Hayworth. The phenomenon was not unlike today's teenage poster craze—where a television star is really more important for the sex appeal she has on a poster than any true ability. (Farrah Fawcett is a prime case in point.) Every star was photographed during World War II but only a handful really made it.

(Top left)
This is the pinup that did not make a star of Betty Grable. Maybe it was the little cat faces over her breasts; maybe the whiskers in her hair. Whatever, she would not make it until two years later.

(Top right)
Susan Hayward was still Edythe Marrener when ordered to pose for this hunk of cheesecake. Later as Susan Hayward, Oscar winner, her skirts stayed firmly around her thespian ankles.

(Right)
Marilyn—not in time for the war. But she quickly became the favorite of the soldiers in Korea.

(Far right)
Rita, her second time out, and a winner; it was hand painted eighteen feet high on a bomber that headed for Berlin. It has since been reproduced in color on the cover of The Great Hollywood Pinups.

(Top Left)
Jean Parker didn't set the world on fire either on the front of lockers or in her career. She did make Power Dive, Torpedo Boat, and I Live On Danger, *all soldier-boy films.*

(Left)
Doris Day thought twice before letting them shoot this picture; she was already a wartime favorite with Les Brown's Band.

(Above right)
Lucy before Desi. A good singer; a good dancer. But her shape didn't make it on the aircraft carriers.

(Far left)
Ava! She was already under contract when this shot showed up on the cover of Stars and Stripes. But it wasn't until then that Louis B. Mayer noticed. "Put her to work," he said.

155

more closely resembled Dorian Gray than those of Robin of Loxeley.)

The national bulletin of the American Legion self-righteously labeled Flynn and Chaplin "but two of the moral lepers being created out in California."

Once again, American newspaper readers began seeing Hollywood as a modern Sodom where booze and broads mixed into an incendiary explosion. A Southern Baptist evangelist, Dr. Robert L. Sumner, totalled up its divorce rate of 1949 vs. its marriage rate. And, said the fire-eater, divorces won it hands-down, 180 to 42. "Friends," he said from the pulpit, "this shameful list of one year's divorces reads exactly like *Who's Who in Hollywood*. Why, friends, Lana Turner has announced that she has bought a home in Nevada so that she can get her divorces quickly and in the comfort of her own bedroom."

Dr. Sumner would probably not have appreciated the humor the Hollywood divorces brought to Santa Monica Superior Court where most of them had their day. The reasons given by the mix-and-match stars were hilarious: Esther Muir charged that Busby Berkeley tore her dress off at a dance; Agnes Miller said Tim McCoy, the cowboy, had "gone Hollywood"; Dorothy Perry accused Stepin Fetchit of wife beating; Mary Poulson said that Bull Montana made faces at her; Bobbe Arnst charged that Johnny Weissmuller moved his brother in to live with them; Vivian Duncan charged that Nils Asther spoke to his mother in Swedish. But these flimsy excuses were good enough for the courtroom by the Pacific. Most of the plaintiffs not only walked out with their freedom but with large handbags full of their spouse's Hollywood loot.

Churches and patriots complained, but, in truth, juicy gossip

Astaire and Garland celebrate Valentine's Day on the Easter Parade set. Astaire, the only impartial party involved in Garland's MGM debacle, said he would come back out of semi-retirement to work with her again . . . "sheer genius," he said.

With Gene Kelly and Van Johnson on the set of the controversial film The Pirate in 1947. No wholly unbiased account of the rigors of this film survives: MGM historians say she went through filming so high on pills that she failed to even remember making some musical numbers.

156

(Above left)
Alice Faye and Phil Harris in the type of chummy family photo that would help Hollywood veer away from elegance to the prosaic and homey image of the fifties. Can Sandra Dee be too far around the corner? Alice was Fox's top canary during the thirties, finally unseated by Betty Grable in the forties (who gave way to Marilyn Monroe in the fifties). Alice and Phil's marriage lasted and is still going strong.

(Above right)
Ozzie and Harriet—when he was still the matinee idol bandleader and she was a blondined "B"-movie star named Harriet Hilliard. After adding David and Ricky they would perpetuate a cozy ruse as the movies' and later televisions' ideal family—living happily behind the picket fence. Only twenty years later would the story come out about the terrible tensions that lurked below the surface of the fatuous family face they presented to the world.

like this was only lubrication to help the money flow faster. In 1948 90 million movie tickets were bought in this country, bringing in $1.9 billion—a record that would not be broken until 1977 when Hollywood had *Star Wars, Close Encounters,* and *Jaws* all circulating at the same time. Star salaries reflected these salad days: In 1948 Crosby got $350,000; Cooper got $300,000; Flynn took home $200,000 (for only three films), and Betty Grable, still America's highest paid woman, made $350,000. Louis B. Mayer, then considered to be the most powerful man in Hollywood, took home the biggest annual paycheck in the country— $1,161,753 (a record he was to hold until the early fifties).

The movie elite had come a long way from its first days in Hollywood when the highest paycheck in town was $5,000 a week, and that going to the only real superstar in 1913—Mary Pickford.

The big bucks rode into town on the war boom and on the strength of a new process—Technicolor—that was suddenly used for most films under the cameras in the mid-forties. It was no longer enough to photograph well or to act well. Suddenly, a star had to have the right color combination. Hair had to match with eyes; skin tone had to blend

Every studio had a dancer; every studio had its operatic soprano; its cowboy. But only MGM had a swimmer—Esther Williams, as powerful an athlete as the movies had seen. Here in the Busby Berkeley finale to one of her films, Esther descends ten stories and then dives from a tower into a lace network of aqua-stars.

Lana Turner, playing herself in the Vincente Minnelli classic, The Bad and the Beautiful. "We took a chance. As the film proceeded, we saw a Lana Turner of great depth materialize on the screen," said Minnelli. It was as perfect an abstract portrait of stardom and the ingratitude of Hollywood as the movies ever achieved. Then Lana had to sit back and watch it come true in her real life.

Robert Stack, as fully packaged a star as Hollywood produced in the forties, is here being taught to fence for a leaden and forgotten movie, The Iron Glove. Stack might have been to the tennis club born, but he fizzled as Columbia's replacement for the fast evaporating Errol Flynn.

with costumes. "In many ways Hollywood acted as hysterical with the coming of color as it had to the coming of sound," said Vincente Minnelli, who would soon be known as the "Technicolor king." "The color technicians were in charge, and they acted like dictators—much as the sound men had ruled in 1928–32."

The most dictatorial of the color-coded bureaucrats was Natalie Kalmus, whose husband Herbert had invented Technicolor in 1915 (and used it himself in an uninspiring feature, *The Gulf Between*). Kalmus, a quiet, dedicated scientist, would have been horrified at his wife's practice of hiring herself out as color consultant on any film that used her late husband's invention. Natalie's Technicolor tyranny caused directors and superstars to gulp bourbon before meeting her on the set. In one instance, Mrs. Kalmus dallied so long before approving the color combinations for the midgets on the *Wizard of Oz* set that their felt costumes began bursting apart under the sweltering lights—sending Judy Garland into fits of giggling.

But her color craziness was catching . . . even established stars had to report to unused sound stages for "tint tests"—with the results being added to the performer's artistic file. Garland, Betty Hutton, and Marlene Dietrich, for instance, were rated as "made for color" while Joan Crawford, Greta Garbo, and Norma Shearer got Ds for drab.

Two of the first stars of the Technicolor era were Betty Grable and Rita Hayworth, pastel pinups whose publicity said they were "discovered overnight." This was more Hollywood fantasy, of course.

Rita, actually a plump cafe dancer named Margarita Cansino, had to hire a press agent to even get a job. And Grable had been working under the name Frances Dean for ten years when Alice Faye's partial retirement resulted in a last-minute assignment in *Down Argentine Way* (but only as a supporting actress for Carmen Miranda, whose tutti-frutti hats made her a Technicolor wonder).

(Right top)
Errol Flynn had a face to melt the Technicolor screen and a grace unseen in the movies since Wally Reid died. And Flynn's career, in a way, was as wasted as Reid's. He cared nothing about acting (or at least said he didn't) and slumbered his way through most parts. "But to the Walter Mittys of this world he was all the heroes in one magnificent, sexy package," said Flynn's boss Jack Warner. After taking unfair flak for not signing up for World War II service, Flynn drifted out in a haze of wenching, boozing, and drugs. He was too much of a gentleman to make an issue of the fact that he had volunteered but was rejected because of a heart defect, malaria, and tuberculosis.

(Right bottom)
Errol, hauled into court by a preposterous teenage duo who said he lured them onto his boat for a midnight orgy, signed autographs in the halls of a Los Angeles court. A scandal that would have toppled a superstar twenty years earlier only made fans eager for more.

Rita's overnight discovery is fairly typical . . . relying as it did on her own clever politics rather than on the wise judgment of Columbia's Harry Cohn, the man gossip columnists applauded for making her a star.

Henry Rogers is actually the man who made Rita a star. And he was an aspiring public relations man, twenty-five years old and trying to get a fingerhold on the Hollywood success ladder. Rogers (now head of the largest PR firm in the industry, Rogers and Cowan) was reportedly playing cards one night with Eddie Judson and his seventeen-year-old wife, Rita Hayworth. Judson, a minor movie wheeler-dealer, began sounding off to Rogers about Rita's option with Columbia Pictures: "We're not getting anywhere, Henry," he said. "Her option's up, and I don't think they're gonna drop her." Rogers put down his cards and began drafting a publicity campaign on a cocktail napkin.

For five percent of Rita's $300-a-week salary, Rogers guaranteed to put her in the headlines. A week later, Rogers went to Gene Herrick, the West Coast editor of *Look* magazine, telling him: "Rita Hayworth is an actress at Columbia who receives a salary of $15,000 a year. And she spends it all on clothes. She thinks that dressing well is the single most important thing for a girl who wants to be a star."

Then Rogers, so the story goes, went downtown to Western Union and sent Rita a telegram naming Hayworth as the best-dressed actress in America—offscreen, of course. He signed it Jackson Carberry, a man who didn't exist, the supposed president of the American Fashion Couturiers Association of America, an organization that didn't exist.

It was good enough for Herrick, and he sent *Look* photographers out to do the spread. Rogers rushed from door to door in Beverly Hills, borrowing a wardrobe—six weeks later she was on the cover . . . the first of fifty-five magazine covers that would eventually be devoted to Rita.

The real PR clincher came when Maggie Maskell, head of magazine publicity for Columbia, brought a *Life* magazine photographer over. Maggie rustled through Hayworth's wardrobe, choosing a pink-and-black nightgown from the rack. "Put this on, get on the bed, give your body a high profile and give me a provocative look."

Before Flynn's visage faded completely from America's movie consciousness, a disturbing shadow, Sean, Errol's son by Lily Damita, reported for work on a sequel to the swashbuckler's most famed role, The Son of Captain Blood. *The film did so-so business, and Flynn Jr. had a try at Zorro. To show how fast the times were changing, Sean announced that acting seemed too insubstantial a career. He trained as a combat photographer and shipped off to Vietnam where he disappeared. (Intelligence officers believe he was killed in Cambodia.)*

The rest is history—the black-and-white pinup would make Rita a Technicolor star.

It was Rita, also, who ushered in a new era of smut by appearing (against her will) on the cover of *Confidential* magazine under the headline, "Dope, Rape and Lawlessness Among Stars."

The magazine threw the public light onto hundreds of scummy stories about the stars—some of them true and many fabricated. Among the truer items were reports on Bob Mitchum's marijuana parties, Steve Cochran's Beverly Hills brawling, and Marie McDonald's run of drunk driving.

This was also the era when the "Hollywood style" of dress (such as Joan Crawford's shoulder pads and Marlene's slacks) of homes (Ozzie and Harriet's ranch-style house) and hair color (such as the platinum hair of Harlow, Grable, and Monroe) would dominate the world. It was possible then and is possible now to find duplicates of Beverly Hills' streets in almost every country-club section of America. When Norma and Constance Talmadge, the silent-era superstar sisters, opened a subdivision of ranch and mission homes in San Diego, contractors across America were flooded with requests for duplicates. (The mini-city in San Diego County was called Talmadge, a cliffside development of movie-set houses by architect Cliff May that sits, unchanged, as a pastel time capsule from the movie years.)

Hollywood stars had the latest in gadgets, the largest of swimming pools, and the earliest solar heaters. But not everything went swimmingly—no matter the money. Consider the monster mansion that William Powell built off the millions he got from *The Thin Man.* Designed by classical architect J.E. Dolena and decorated by Jean Harlow (Powell's girlfriend at the time), the house had buttons that could open and shut all the doors and featured a bar that could be turned into a barbecue with a hidden button. When it worked, the spit rose from the floor and the charcoal burners emerged noiselessly from a closet. "I built a house

Gloria Swanson descends the staircase of a Hollywood Mansion in 1950's Sunset Boulevard, *a movie depicting Hollywood's death.*

of dreams, but it turned into a devilish monster," said Powell. "I would push one button to go into the parlor and find myself in the kitchen. There were thirty-two rooms in the house, and something unexpected was happening in every one of them."

The homes of nonmovie millionaires such as Carrie Guggenheim and Edward Doheny added further to the bizarre atmosphere of the movie capital. As for the commerical buildings, magnates like Sid Grauman and Max Factor hired actual set decorators (moonlighting from the studios) to design the accoutrements for their skyscrapers. "By merely showing these buildings in film after film, the movies not only created a real estate boom; they spread a style," said film historian Kevin Brownlow. This helps explain why the Left Bank Cafeteria in Paris looks like an Astaire and Rogers set and why statues of Jean Harlow hold up a buffet table in Rome's Cine Tratorria.

The wire services and fan magazines dispensed photos and stories that George Bernard Shaw called "popcorn of the mind." Rita choosing a gardenia, Crawford picking out a baby lion at the Farmers Market; Cornel Wilde building his biceps on the beach at Malibu—it looked as if Hollywood would drift off to eternity sipping a daiquiri, wearing a $300 suit, and colored by a flamingo Pacific sunset.

Then came two sociological and one legal earthquake—television, the House UnAmerican Activites Committee, and a government

Eddie puts lipstick on for Debbie as the two prepare for an appearance on Fisher's "Coke Time." Liz was still safely married to Mike Todd, and nobody had mentioned Cleopatra *yet.*

162

One thing and one thing only compensated for the loss of glamour—the enormous gains in film technology. Here, Alfred Hitchcock races ahead of Cary Grant who in turn is pursued by a sinister airplane in North by Northwest. Such shots would have been unthinkable even five years before.

antitrust ruling that forced the studios to sell off their nationwide networks of movie theaters. The first and the third would undermine Hollywood's financial security, and the second would brutally wound its soul.

And they all came at once.

Hollywood had known about television for years—even watched cheerfully as General David Sarnoff put out a test broadcast of a Rudy Vallee show in 1937. But in the thirties the movie industry, which called TV "radiomovies," laughed at it. "Nobody will ever stay home and watch those little 'radiomovies'," said Goldwyn—who was also the man who said he wouldn't believe Technicolor until "I see it in black and white."

If TV was a threat to the movies, it would already have become so—said the movie moguls. After all, it had been around for about twenty years. Nobody noticed that for twelve years the Federal Communications Commission had limited the manufacture of receivers—waiting first for tests to be finished and then holding back because of weapons production during World War II.

The FCC dropped all restrictions in 1948 . . . by 1949 there were a million TV sets in American homes; by 1950 there were ten million. The people who went to the movies in incredible numbers began staying

(Left)
Judy and Mickey after a tense day on the set of their latest Andy Hardy movie—Babes on Broadway. A masseuse tries to ease Judy's tension, and the weariness shows on their faces. (Sometimes they worked on three pictures concurrently.)

(Right)
The worry may not entirely show on her face on the set of Easter Parade with co-star Fred Astaire and visitor Ricardo Montalban (now of "Fantasy Island.") This was the last truly sane cinema achievement for Judy at MGM . . . a trail of broken movies followed.

(Opposite Top)
The irrepressible munchkins surround Judy and technical directors on the first day of shooting for Oz. The midgets, virtually every findable small person in America, were mischievious, but so was Judy. "We could hardly share an off-color joke without seeing her sneak up to listen—then repeat," said Bert Lahr, the Cowardly Lion. "Absolutely precocious."

(Opposite left)
Judy and Mrs. Frank L. Baum, widow of the author of The Wizard of Oz. MGM pretended for all the world that they hand selected Garland to play Dorothy. They really wanted Shirley Temple, of course, and they waited and waited until Judy was almost too old to play the role. (She was seventeen when they finally started the cameras.)

What's wrong with this picture? Easy, the smiles. Usually blows and angry words were flying between the movies' handsome Tarzan, Johnny Weissmuller and off-and-on wife Lupe Velez. Mrs. Frank Borzage, owner of this Hawaiian Paradise Club, is in the center. Lupe sent Johnny a pair of white kid boxing gloves after one month-long fight with the inscription: "Darling, so you can punch me if I leave you again." Lupe Velez drifted onto Hollywood's dark side after divorcing Tarzan and, in 1944, had her hairdresser and makeup man over, sent herself a roomful of flowers, dressed in an evening gown, and swallowed a vial of pills—dying gracefully two hours later.

John Garfield, perhaps the ultimate victim of the political purge of the late forties and early fifties. He died of a heart attack the night before he was due to testify in front of the House UnAmerican Activities Committee. That tragedy never even needed comment; still doesn't.

The city's new glamour of the fifties began to have a harder, flint-edged look—typified by this shot of Fred Astaire and Cyd Charisse made for The Bandwagon, *1953. Charisse would later tell of the six weeks of torturous rehearsal that Astaire demanded before the photographers were let in. It sure looked pretty, but the fun seemed to be gone.*

home—watching Lucille Ball and other Hollywood stars who went over to the enemy. It was bad enough in New York and Los Angeles—the big cities. But, like lightning, television raided the audience in the small towns, the mainstay of the movies, and the number of stations jumped from 617 to 1,298 in only twelve months.

Between 1948 and 1952 Hollywood saw movie profits drop $500 million while the average weekly attendance dropped from 90 million to 46 million. And the bigger studios were hit hardest. Profits at MGM dropped from $17.9 million in 1946 to $4.2 million in 1949, and Fox dropped from $22 million in 1946 to $4.2 million in 1951.

An eight-point earthquake couldn't have done as much damage.

Hollywood frantically turned to technology as they had during the talkie hysteria. They tried 3D, but when audiences had the choice of 3D or regular (as with *Kiss Me Kate* which was issued in both versions), they bought tickets to the regular versions. They tried wide screen, curved screen, and double screen—stereo sound and wraparound sound and even, in the case of Mike Todd, "smellavision" which sent out odors to match the action on the screen. After spending $6 million to perfect his scented movie projector, Todd previewed it with a "smella-vision" film, *The Scent of Mystery.* But as the odors of chocolate, rum,

(Opposite right)
Television, which introduced the scent of fear to Hollywood's executive lunchrooms, also caused the studios to ruthlessly exploit their most proven artists—such as Cyd Charisse, hanging from a wire as "Miss New Year, 1952." In April MGM stuffed her into a monkey-fur suit with white ears as "The Easter Bunny." Her friends like Astaire and Gene Kelly could only blush and look the other way.

Four little contract players all in a line—Freddie Bartholomew, Academy Award winner Mary Astor, Judy, and Walter Pidgeon. "We did what we were told," said Bartholomew years later when he was safely out of Hollywood and a successful advertising executive. Astor, put under contract right after her Oscar, came onto the lot and was told she would be playing Judy's mother the next day. "What about the script," she said. "Don't worry your head about that," came the answer. "So much for the power and glory of the Oscar," she said.

Television crept up on the movies. It seemed too little and creaky in the early black-and-white days— more like a family chat. (Here Groucho and crew prepare for a telecast of "You Bet Your Life.") So the city slumbered. . . . "It shows the arrogance of movies. They felt so secure that TV could never affect them," said Ed Sullivan. "They had learned nothing from the death of silent films or the impact of radio."

and carnations drifted out over the New York crowd, people got up and left. "I think the popcorn smell is better," said one disgruntled patron. "Smells indeed."

To make matters worse, in the late forties the courts ordered the studios to divest themselves of their large theater chains. Until then they virtually monopolized the distribution and exhibition of films across America . . . Loew's, Orpheum, RKO. Pity the budding independent producer who wished to break away from studio ties. No theater, no show! The effect of the divestiture ruling was far reaching, paving the way for the independents, stars-turned-producers, and production in Europe and elsewhere at nonunion wages.

The extravagant days seemed gone forever. When Judy Garland, older and under pressure to revive a flagging career, collapsed and needed stimulants to get her through, MGM sacked her. When Vincente Minnelli wanted to film *Brigadoon* in the real Scottish heather, Dore Schary told him to spray California flowers purple. When Sterling Hayden made the swashbuckling *Golden Hawk,* the studio just spliced old *Spanish Main* footage into the background. Big stars like Lana Turner, Ava Gardner, Robert Taylor, and even Clark Gable were shoved out of their contracts.

"It seemed like the studio was falling down around us," said Debbie Reynolds, who had only been discovered on a Burbank high school stage in 1948. "I got in on the last several years of the big musicals. And then it was over—we were out on our ears. And it especially hurt the women—we couldn't really become producers or directors then. Luckily, I got a second wind from Howard Hughes—others weren't so lucky."

Just as suddenly, movie fans had no time for glamour. The new stars—Rock Hudson and Steve McQueen—wore jeans and drank milk. Doris Day and Sandra Dee didn't even wear makeup. And the biggest new name in entertainment had never even owned a suit or ridden in a new car. But Hollywood would have to deal with this new star and others like him because in less than ten years these newcomers would rule the roost. Particularly this new star. His name? Elvis Presley.

Elvis helped to fill what was by then a vacuum in the galaxy of stars. By the time MGM brought him out to Hollywood and gave him the key to the studio, Hollywood had already been badly damaged by the Communist scare brought to town by the House UnAmerican Activities Committee.

The furor had started innocently in the Hollywood of the thirties. And it started with idealistic stars, writers, and directors who formed the Hollywood for Roosevelt Committee in 1936.

After Pearl Harbor, this group was expanded to form the nucleus of the Hollywood Independent Citizens Committee for Arts, Services, and Professions. From that launching pad, left-leaning actors and writers

TV cameras sneak right up to the gates of the studios (as here at Paramount) like the wolf in "Little Red Riding Hood." The studios welcomed them, often supplying free talent, until the men back on Wall Street said: "Hey, look what's happening to your ticket sales, you schmucks . . . everybody's staying home."

The Larry Parks story assumed the proportions of a Greek tragedy when the actor was hauled before the House UnAmerican Activities Committee and ordered to tell all; to name names. From the distance of thirty years it seems clear that Parks, hounded by his studio, his attorneys, and his agents, believed he had to turn over the names of his fellow Hollywood Communists of a decade earlier. But first he looked up and said: "Don't make me crawl in the mud . . . don't." Then he quietly began calling the role.

(Right)
Parks, here in Nazi uniform for 1942's The Black Parachute, was through in Hollywood from his first words into the Washington D.C. microphone. He got off the plane in Los Angeles to read the headline: "Jolson Sings Again," referring to his testimony back in Washington. Columbia bought out his contract; he was blacklisted and, worse, counter-blacklisted by the liberals who might have helped him.

drifted into local cells of the American Communist Party. Most of them joined in a fervor of patriotism when Russia became our wartime ally. After all, the Nazis and the Japanese were the bad guys. Roosevelt and Churchill were shown in league with Stalin at wartime conferences in newsreels across the country. Why should less be expected of Hollywood?

However, not even film careers can be as uncertain as politics. Within a year of V-J Day, the alliance had fallen apart and within five years the FBI, congressional investigators, and right-wing volunteers would accuse the left-wing artists of bending Hollywood's movie output in such a way that America was "forced" into the war on the side of Russia. Further, the accusers, Senator Joe McCarthy the loudest among them, charged "Tinseltown pinks" with debasing America and glorifying Russia in the films they wrote, directed, or acted in. (Never mind that most of those on the pinko lists had never been involved with anything more sinister than The Beautiful Blonde from Bashful Bend.)

The anticommunists, working over a period of five years, called hundreds of actors, writers, and directors before their public hearings—dividing them into groups of "friendly" witnesses and "unfriendly" witnesses. As actor after actor trudged to Washington, friendly came to mean stoolie (men and women who gave lists of friends to Congress as "possible suspects") and unfriendly came to mean "Red" and "traitor."

It was suddenly an era of lists, with former FBI agents publishing Red Channels, a complete guide, supposedly, of commies in Hollywood; and American Legion execs writing Red Star over Hollywood—A Public List of Entertainment Traitors.

The pudgy men in flappy gray suits even bedded down in those bastions of Hollywood elegance—the Chateau Marmont and the Garden of Allah—meeting in dark cocktail corners with informants such as Hedda Hopper and Adolphe Menjou, two who didn't wait for summonses—they hand-carried their sacrificial names right to the top.

"Nobody who didn't go through it could understand the level of panic and raw fear that was alive here," said publicist Henry Rogers, who stuck by his friend, Oscar-winner Carl Foreman, even after a year of angry threats from Hedda Hopper and John Wayne. "People whose names appeared on those lists, even if they were innocent, could literally have the food taken off their tables," said Rogers—a man whom Hedda vowed she would run out of town.

"To us liberals then, planned investigations into the lives of our colleagues, even those we did not consider close friends, were alarming and required our opposition," said Dore Schary, the major power at MGM during those years.

By late 1951 three different groups of Hollywood voyagers had made the trip to Capitol Hill—those who took the Fifth Amendment and went to jail; those who informed on their friends and fellow artists; and those who stood up to the committee, keeping their integrity—but usually not their jobs.

Ironically, those who became stoolies fared the worst. For instance, Larry Parks, the actor who had scored the greatest career break-

through with *The Jolson Story* pleaded with the committee: "Don't made me crawl in the mud . . . don't." Then his words trailed off. And his eyes got moist.

The committee rephrased the question: "Who were the members of the Communist Party Cell to which you were assigned?" There was a pause—a silence that filled the chamber. Then, in a hoarse voice, Parks began his list: "Lee J. Cobb, Dorothy Tree, Gale Sondergaard, Anne Revere."

Two days later, Columbia tore up Parks' $75,000 contract for a picture he had already started. A week after that, Columbia President Harry Cohn bought out his contract. "We picked that kid up off the street," said Cohn. "We got a traitor."

When Parks arrived by train in Los Angeles, the afternoon newspaper headline said: "Jolson Sings Again." Parks' loss was to be complete. He would play only one more role, a cameo in 1965 for his friend John Huston.

Clubbing Parks when he was down, Hedda wrote, "The life of one American soldier is worth all the careers in Hollywood. To Hell with Parks and all those late confessors. Parks should have made a public confession for his sins. This one was forced."

Sterling Hayden, Lee J. Cobb, and almost a score of others were interrogated before Congress for a list.

John Wayne, Hedda, and others were banded together into the 1,000-member Motion Picture Alliance which said, in its by-laws, "We do not publicly associate with traitors."

Adolphe in his early days as a leading man in silent films (His Private Life). He had billed himself as "the gentleman actor," one of the best dressed, most cultivated men in America, welcome in the homes of Hollywood's finest. Some of these hosts, particularly one director, would hear their dinner conversations aired before Congress as evidence of their alleged Communist leanings.

(Opposite left)
Adolphe Menjou volunteered to inform on his peers. "Menjou and the others," writes screenwriter and director Philip Dunne in his new book, Take Two, *"provided the . . . names of the people they thought were Communists, had heard were Communists; looked like Communists, and associated with Communists, sympathized with Communists or whose behavior was simply too liberal for their peculiar tastes."*

(Below)
Menjou adds addenda to his testimony before HUAC. The gate that he opened also admitted the voices of others.

"Run 'em out of town," said Menjou.

The American Legion began running lists of films to be boycotted by patriots: *Death of A Salesman, A Streetcar Named Desire, A Place In the Sun.* . . .

Some of Hollywood's greatest heroes found it hard to be either strong or silent. Take the case of Gary Cooper. Coop badly wanted to rescue his friend, Carl Foreman, the man who was working on the script for *High Noon* when the hearings started. Foreman took the Fifth and refused to name names.

The writer got back to town in time to read newspaper headlines stating that his closest friend, director Stanley Kramer, had fired him for the film company he headed. "Those of us who knew how close Kramer and Foreman had been were shocked to see that," said Rogers, who threw his public relations company squarely behind Foreman. "But husbands and wives in Hollywood argued all night, asking, 'whose side are you on?'"

Cooper had also read the headline and called Foreman up with a proposition. "I know you're forming a company to fight the blacklist, and I want in," said Coop. Rogers then agreed to do the publicity campaign for a fee to be paid later.

Two days later, *The Hollywood Reporter* announced that Cooper, Rogers, and Foreman were all directors in the new Carl Foreman Productions. So far, so good. Rogers got home from work that day almost shell-shocked by calls from Hedda and dozens of others who said, in essence, "I didn't know you were a Commie TOO."

Even Sterling Hayden, catapulted to fame as Paramount's "blond Viking God," was cowed by HUAC, finally naming names and trying to duck a courageous stint helping partisans in Yugoslavia during World War II.

(Below)
The strain and early aging shows on Hayden's face as he sits with his wife Betty after caving in before the committee. Much later, in a brilliant book, Hayden revealed his personal and private grief over what he had done, depicting himself as a far worse villain than he was.

There was worse to come. Cooper, who was up in Montana hunting with Ernest Hemmingway, found a boxful of telegrams outside his tent—a day later. Warner Brothers was trying to break his contract using the "morals clause," Louis B. Mayer sent stern warnings, and a favorite Cooper director, Walter Wanger, sent a bullying message. Three days later Cooper, still in Montana, caved in.

Rogers sadly drafted a press release. "Mr. Cooper has the highest regard for Carl Foreman's talents, his integrity and his character, but, as a result of pressures that have been applied, I am forced to submit my resignation as a member of the board of directors of Carl Foreman Productions.

The day of the press conference, Rogers was threatened by seven of his clients, by an important business manager who had sent him ten clients, and from an even more hysterical Hedda Hopper.

"God, it sounded like a scene from a 'B' movie," said Rogers. But he held firm. And it was Wayne, Hopper, and the Hollywood right-wing that gave in—paving the way for Rogers and Cowan to become one of the most successful public relations agencies in the country.

"It's funny how a man just holding his integrity was suddenly labeled a hero," said Rogers.

On a higher level, the Hollywood bosses met at a summit conference in New York—with Schenk, Mayer, and Jack Warner present. Men who had built film empires from scratch suddenly had too much to lose.

Marsha Hunt, a fast rising MGM star, (here with Gene Kelly and Franchot Tone in a patriotic film) was one of the many caught in the rapidly expanding blacklist.

Hitler's Children, a blatant but expectable antiNazi film made during the war with Bonita Granville, was one of many supposed examples of Communist infiltration of the movies.

The fabulous Mocambo, neighboring nightclub to the Trocadero on the Sunset Strip, vied with the Troc for star-studded popularity. While the Troc had a breathtaking view of the lowlands south of the Strip, Mocambo had both the view and a long glass enclosure in front of it which was alive with dozens of parrots and macaws in fascinating motion. Typical of all first-class Sunset Boulevard bistros, men were required to wear jackets and ties; women in slacks were refused admittance. So were men alone, and women alone. Obvious hustling at the bar, either sex, subjected the perpetrator to quietly unobtrusive eviction.

Schary, who was a voting member of the mogul trust, said: "All I could do was form a minority opinion and then try to help the guilds form a barrier against wholesale firings." Back from the coast, Schary's secretary laid the newspaper on his desk: "Studio Head Says He Will Hire Reds."

After that, Hollywood's major organizations joined in the search—with the Screen Actor's Guild and the Motion Picture Academy of Arts and Sciences condemning what both groups referred to as conspirators. For five years after, Oscar winners had to swear that "I am not now, nor have I ever been a member of the Communist Party."

Writers Carl Foreman and Dalton Trumbo were to later have triumphs when, writing under other names on the artistic black market, each won an Oscar for best screenplay. (Trumbo finally collected his, but Foreman is still fighting the battle for his.)

Trumbo, writing about these events which ended Hollywood's golden age as surely as a coffin nail, said: "When you who are in your forties now or younger look back with curiosity at Hollywood's dark time, as I sincerely think you should—it will do no good to search for villains because there were none. There were only victims."

In many ways, that applies to all of Hollywood's tragedies.

NBC, the old studios in downtown Hollywood. Not much to look at; not much action. In contrast to the vibrant activity of the studio days, this palace of tape pushers is a mockery of a once great city.

VII REQUIEM FOR TINSELTOWN

August 3, 1963: "She was found in bed this morning in her home in Hollywood only a mile or two away, but a social universe away, from the place where she was born thirty-six years ago as Norma Jean Baker. She died with a bottle of barbiturates at her elbow."

Marilyn Monroe, the world's most desired woman, was home on Saturday night without a date.

Of course people had stopped believing in the old Hollywood dream long before Monroe died. The dream had tarnished, withered, and then died as the legends shriveled up like the witch in *The Wizard Of Oz*.

By the sixties even nostalgia was becoming tattered. Growing old, the town took on some ugly wrinkles—the neon of porn palaces on The Boulevard, the hippie invasion, and the virus of the drug scene. The searchlights still stabbed into the sky. But when you traced them down they might be found in the parking lot of a supermarket advertising a weekend special on canned corn.

There were still premières. But most of the stars stayed home or were living in New York, London, or Rome. The town as it once was had become a giant haunted house where the ghosts of the past, whose names are lettered in brass on the sidewalks of Hollywood Boulevard,

Capitol Records, the centerpiece of new Hollywood—where recording stars just off the bus from Nashville took over the mansions of the languid stars of the gilded era.

Hollywood Boulevard during its zenith—the forties. It was an era of familiar glamour in the small town atmosphere of the boulevard— Greer Garson and Irene Dunne traded gossip as they bought hats; Merle Oberon dashed into Max Factor's for a weekly facial and Marlene Dietrich still wore shoulder furs to luncheon. Even then some Hollywood institutions were in their sunset years—like the Hollywood Hotel (draped in palms in the foreground) and the Misses Janes School, hidden behind the white bank tower. Just around the corner was the era of plastic signs, adult sex cinemas, and deterioration. "We just sat by and let it happen," said Mary Pickford. "Weren't we foolish? What a tawdry monument we left."

were like mirages of a time long gone.

On the Sunset Strip the glamorous clubs shut down and the street literally belonged to the recording industry.

Then even the old legends died. As Charles Higham recounts in his book *Celebrity Circus,* when he went to interview Mary Pickford in 1969 he was shown into the cavernous living room where all of Hollywood's royalty had passed over the years. He was deposited next to a phone which began ringing. Finally, he answered it.

"Welcome to Pickfair," said the voice from above. "Look to your left," said the voice. "You see that table with the lamp on it? There's an ivory-colored book on the table. Why don't you pick it up and bring it over to the phone. Now turn to page 21."

Higham leafed through the book, finding pictures of Lord and Lady Mountbatten. The voice began again: "You see, Lord and Lady Mountbatten stayed with us. They were so charming. Being British, I thought you'd appreciate it. It's been nice talking to you. Good-bye."

Then Mary Pickford hung up her phone next to her bed somewhere far up in the mansion.

Higham was shown to the door.

"Nice to have had you," said the butler. "Come again."

(Above)
Hollywood Paradox: While legitimate theatres in other parts of the country have gone to the movies, the celebrated home of the Academy Awards for many years has successfully gone legit. Its historical Art Deco interiors are monumental and their preservation at least temporarily assured.

(Far left)
Summer fireworks and the Los Angeles Philharmonic at the Hollywood Bowl. Almost sixty years later it still provides one of the most delightful evenings under the stars with everything from Beverly Sills to some of the best jazz concerts on the West Coast.

(Left)
On the stage of the Pantages in Sugar Babies, Spring 1980, two who survived (endured): intrepid, indestructible Anne Miller (not a hair out of place after a half-century of tap dancing) and still effervescent Mickey Rooney.

179

Hollywood in 1915—room for a dream to grow, with orange-scented air backdropped by eternally blue skies against snowcapped mountains.

Hollywood in the sixties—a rare clear view on a smog-free day.

The spectacular "blue whale," alias the Pacific Design Center, backdropped by the Sunset Strip and the Hollywood hills. It sits a short block from the intersection of Palm Avenue and Santa Monica Boulevard (the 1892 railroad junction of Sherman, page 52) where it showcases most of the top design lines in the country.

And so the cavalcade passed. What does one say of Hollywood today, dateline 1980? It depends on whether one is talking about The Land or The Legend.

Hollywood, The Land, has become a small, but very expensive parcel of acreage on the tax assessor's map of a very large city, strategically squeezed between the mother lode of Beverly Hills and downtown Los Angeles. The real estate boom of the seventies swept away much of the urban decay. One era has passed away and another is beginning. The king is dead, long live the king!

Today the movie stars are slowly moving back along Mulholland Drive and the green, quiet country roads. The canyons are inhabited by recording stars, the pop industry owns the Strip. So, in a sense, the Hollywood Hills are alive with the sound of music.

On LaBrea Avenue, A & M Records has built a glistening, multimillion dollar Art Deco recording complex south of Sunset Boulevard at the site of the original Chaplin studio, gracefully incorporating and

Despite the blight of tasteless billboards flanking her base and impairing her view, the Chateau Marmont maintains the haughty image which has lured the biggest names in show business into temporary or long-term residence since 1927. Here's where Jean Harlow and Hal Rossen honeymooned; where Joanne Woodward and Paul Newman met; where an outgoing young Howard Hughes had a suite; where Sophia Loren, Marcello Mastroianni, Marcel Marceau, Marilyn Monroe, Lawrence Olivier, Clark Gable and Bea Lillie stayed. But only the great Greta Garbo, who lived here, ever slept in the dining room in her own bed after moving in there to escape the party noises from a neighboring suite! The final blow was a twirling ice skater to ballyhoo a Las Vegas hotel.

Charlie Chaplin in 1915 when Sarah Bernhardt called him the first true romantic since Lord Byron. The trusting look would age into a painful awareness of the loss of innocence. The Little Tramp did not get a star on Hollywood Boulevard until the seventies—and then only after a fight by local fans.

(Above right)
Marilyn! The day she was fired by Twentieth Century Fox—only a wistful shadow of her former vitality remains. Director George Cukor ordered this picture for a color and lighting test, but even he admitted that it was impossible to continue. "It was no use, she was too sick," said Cukor years later. Two weeks later, Marilyn died in the moist pre-dawn darkness of luxurious Brentwood—America's most desirable woman—without a date on a Saturday night.

preserving it. In Griffith Park, the Greek Theatre plays to capacity audiences, and on hot summer nights the Los Angeles Philharmonic packs in crowds complete with picnic baskets and wine coolers at the Hollywood Bowl. On Hollywood Boulevard, the Pantages Theatre, site of some of the greatest premières and an architectural masterpiece, has gone legit with "the best of Broadway."

To the west, the mammoth, glass-sheathed Pacific Design Center rises up like a great blue whale where the cowboy bandit Tiburcio Vasquez rode and romanced a century ago. And to the north, John Travolta carries on the same (though urbanized) romantic tradition as he presses his boots into wet cement at the Chinese Theatre amidst swooning fans.

We like to think that Daeida Hartell Wilcox with her shrewd eye for propriety and property, were she sitting today, harp in hand, atop Mount Lee, would not be entirely displeased with the renaissance below.

And what of Hollywood, The Legend? It never has, nor will it ever die. There are few people in the world—from Sri Lanka to Zim-

Ciro's sign; only a photographic souvenir now. During the glamour years of the Sunset Strip from the mid-30s until the onslaught of television, it was the chic and elegant playground of the stars along with the Mocambo and the "Troc," also long gone.

babwe, Brazilia to Beijing—who have not heard of it, thought of it, and perhaps incorporated it in their dreams. What do they think? Possibly it is their own secret never-never land, born in fantasy, awash in glamour, and nourished on the magic of film. Perhaps the name alone is a touchstone for awakening the universal Walter Mitty in all of us, providing us with an inner strength for getting through.

They have put the Hollywood Sign back on Mount Lee shinier and brighter than ever. The buses, planes, trains, and tours pour in from all over the world to seek out the footprints in the cement at the Chinese Theatre, take a Universal tour, peer and be photographed (with mixed emotions) at Hollywood and Vine, be bussed by the homes of the great, the nearly great, and the former great, real or imagined.

Seventy years after it all began it is still one of the best shows in the country . . . still playing to capacity audiences and probably always will.

Fade out, rising music and . . .

. . . The End

Sid Grauman's publicity gimmick which became a world famous tradition is still one of the greatest shows in town. Here John Travolta leaves his bootmarks in the cement next to imprints of Betty Grable's leg, Al Jolson's knee and Jimmy Durante's nose.

Selected Bibliography

Andrews, Bart. *The Story of "I Love Lucy."* Popular Books, 1976.
        The inside look at the founding of a TV series.

Anger, Kenneth. *Hollywood Babylon.* Straight Arrow Books, 1975.
        Interesting subject matter—touches on some subjects not covered by other books—but highly inaccurate in parts.

Arce, Hector. *The Secret Life of Tyrone Power.* Bantam Books, 1979.
        New facts about Power and the era in which he worked.

Ashley, Elizabeth. *Actress: Postcards From the Road.* Fawcett-Crest, 1978.

Astor, Mary. *A Life on Film.* Dell Books, 1967.
        The classic book on silent films—told by a star.

Austin, John. *Hollywood's Unsolved Mysteries.* Ace Publishing Co., 1970.

Bacall, Lauren. *By Myself.* Ballantine Books, 1978.

Baxter, John. *Hollywood in the Thirties.* A.S. Barnes & Co., 1968.
        A very general overview of the decade.

————. *Sixty Years of Hollywood.* A.S. Barnes & Co., 1973.
        Sketchy account of Hollywood and its rumors.

Best of Life. Time/Life Publications, 1973.

Blum, Daniel. *A Pictorial History of the Silent Screen.* Grosset & Dunlap, 1953.
        Wonderful account, movie-by-movie, of the silents.

Bosworth, Patricia. *Montgomery Clift.* Bantam Books, 1978.

Bowser, Eileen, ed. *Film Notes.* Museum of Modern Art, 1969.

Brenner, Marie. *Going Hollywood.* Dell Books, 1976.

Brownlow, Kevin. *Hollywood, The Pioneers.* Alfred Knopf, Inc., 1979.
        The most beautiful and complete book on any era in Hollywood history yet published. A tour de force with intricate facts.

————. *The Parade's Gone By . . . .* Brown Publishers, 1968.
        Marvelous book—with 500 pages of original research on the making of silent films.

Ceplair, Larry and Englund, Steven. *The Inquisition in Hollywood.* Doubleday, 1979.

Clooney, Rosemary. *This for Remembrance.* Playboy Press, 1977.

Coleberd, Frances. *Adventures in California: A Recreation Guide to the Golden State.* Library of Congress, 1976.

Crawford, Christina. *Mommie Dearest.* Berkley Books, 1978.

Davies, Marion. *The Times We Had.* Ballantine Books, 1975.

Dietz, Howard. *Dancing in the Dark.* Bantam Books, 1974.

Dunleavy, Steve. *Elvis: What Happened?* Ballantine Books, 1977.

Fairbanks, Douglas, Jr. and Schickel, Richard. *The Fairbanks Album.* Little, Brown & Co., 1975.
        Moody and sensitive portrait of life with Hollywood's most famous family.

Farmer, Frances. *Will There Really Be A Morning?* Dell Books, 1972.

Finch, Christopher and Rosenkrantz, Linda. *Gone Hollywood.* Doubleday, 1979.

Flynn, Errol. *My Wicked, Wicked Ways.* G.P. Putnam & Sons, 1959.
> *Autobiography that is full of inaccuracies and misinformation.*

Fontaine, Joan. *No Bed of Roses.* Berkley Books, 1979.

Freedland, Michael. *The Two Lives of Errol Flynn.* Bantam Books, 1980.

Gebhard, David and von Breton, Harriette. *L.A. in the Thirties: 1931–1941.* Peregrine Smith, Inc., 1975.

Griffith, Richard and Mayer, Arthur. *The Movies.* Simon & Schuster, 1957.
> *General account of movie genres—rare pictures.*

Halberstam, David. *The Powers That Be.* Alfred A. Knopf, 1979.

Hayne, Donald, ed. *Cecil B. De Mille's Autobiography.* Prentice-Hall, Inc., 1959.
> *Detailed look at the world as dictated by De Mille.*

Hayward, Brooke. *Haywire.* Bantam Books, 1977.

Hellman, Lillian. *Pentimento.* Signet Books, 1973.

———. *Scoundrel Time.* Little, Brown & Co., 1976.
> *Painful but accurate look at Hollywood's most shameful era.*

Heston, Charlton. *Charlton Heston: The Actor's Life Journals* 1956–1976. Pocket Books, 1976.

Herman, Hal C., ed. *How I Broke Into the Movies.* Hal C. Herman, 1929.

Hirschorn, Clive. *The Warner Brothers Story.* Crown Publishers, Inc., 1979.

Historic Decade 1950–1960. YEAR, Inc., Baldwin H. Ward, 1960.

Hopkins, Jerry. *Elvis.* Warner, 1972.

Hotchner, A.E. *Doris Day: Her Own Story.* Bantam Books, 1975.

Kaminsky, Stuart M. *Coop: The Life & Legend of Gary Cooper.* St. Martin's Press, 1980.

Kanin, Garson. *Hollywood.* Viking Press, 1974.

———. *Moviola.* Simon & Schuster, 1979.

Keylin, Arleen, ed. *Hollywood Album Two, The New York Times.* Arno Press, 1979.
> *Interesting obituaries of hundreds of stars—fine details.*

Koopal, Grace G. *Free Enterprise, Foundation of America's Greatness: A Biography of Charles E. Toberman.* Anderson, Ritchie & Simon, 1970.

Levy, Alan. *Forever, Sophia.* Grosset & Dunlap, Inc., 1979.

Life Goes to the Movies. Time/Life Publications, 1975.

Lind, Margot and Rapaport, Roger. *The California Catalogue.* Library of Congress, 1977.

Linet, Beverly. *Ladd, A Hollywood Tragedy.* Berkley Books, 1979.

Longstreet, Stephen. *All Star Cast: An Anecdotal History of Los Angeles.* Thomas Y. Crowell Co., 1977.

Maltin, Leonard. *The Real Stars.* Popular Books, 1979.

_____ . *TV Movies*. 1979–1980 Edition. Signet Books, 1978.

Marx, Arthur. *Goldwyn*. Ballantine Books, 1976.

Masquers Golden Anniversary: "The Jester," 1925–1975. The Masquers Club, 1975.

Minnelli, Vincente. *I Remember It Well*. Berkley Books, 1974.

Morella, Joe & Epstein, Ed. *The IT Girl*. Dell Books, 1976.

McClelland, Doug. *Susan Hayward*. Pinnacle Books, 1973.

Newmark, Harris. *Sixty Years In Southern California: 1853–1913*. Zeitlin & Ver Brugge, 1970.
                         Wonderful early history of the land and the city.

Osborne, Robert. *Fifty Golden Years of Oscar*. Ese California, 1979.

Palmer, Edwin O. *Hollywood History*. Edwin O. Palmer, 1937.
                         Rare, somewhat outdated look at early Hollywood—from pioneer's viewpoint.

Pepitone, Lena and Stadiem, William. *Marilyn Monroe Confidential*. Pocket Books, 1980.

Rogers, Harry. *Walking the Tightrope*. William Morrow & Co., 1980.

Roth, Johnny. *The Hollywood Hall of Fame*. Richards Enterprises, 1968.

Roud, Richard. *Cinema: A Critical Dictionary*. Viking Press, 1980.

Rovin, Jeff. *Book of Movie Lists*. Signet Books, 1979.

Shale, Richard. *Academy Awards*. Ungar Publishing Co., 1978.

Shulman, Irving. *Valentino*. Trident Press, 1967.

Signoret, Simone. *Nostalgia Isn't What It Used to Be*. Penguin Books, 1979.

Steinberg, Cobbett. *Reel Facts: The Movie Book of Records*. Random House, 1978.
                         The best source of raw data on box office receipts, awards, and studio financing.

Strait, Raymond. *Mrs. Howard Hughes*. Holloway House, 1970.

Thomas, Bob. *Joan Crawford*. Bantam Books, 1978.

Tierney, Gene. *Self Portrait*. Berkley Books, 1980.

Torrence, Bruce. *Hollywood, The First 100 Years*. Hollywood Chamber of Commerce and Fiske
Enterprises, 1979.
                         The only true history of Hollywood buildings.

Tryon, Thomas. *Crowned Heads*. Fawcett Publications, 1976.

Vallee, Rudy. *Let the Chips Fall . . . .* Stackpole Books, 1975.

Van Daalen, Nicholas. *The Complete Book of Movie Lists*. Pagurian Press, 1979.

Walker, Alexander. *The Shattered Silents*. William Morrow & Co., 1979.
                         The best, most comprehensive book on the coming of sound and its aftermath.

Watkins, T.H. *California: An Illustrated History*. American West Publishing Co., 1973.

Weaver, John D. *El Pueblo Grande: A Non-Fiction Book About Los Angeles*. Anderson, Ritchie & Simon, 1973.

Index

A finale. Douglas Fairbanks and Mary Pickford in silent movies' sunset year; he in costume for The Black Pirate— *she dressed for her film,* Sparrows. *Their glory days were over—a young flock of talking stars were banging at the gates of the studios.*